How to Speak to Anyone

Master Public Speaking, How to Communicate Effectively, Speak Confidently With Anyone

Larin Carney

Table of Contents

Introduction

My grandfather, a wise and gentle soul, would often impart his wisdom to me during our cherished moments together. One particular piece of advice he shared has resonated with me throughout my life. "Sender," he would say, "communication does not work when two people speak at the same time." As a young and somewhat naïve boy, I struggled to fully comprehend the profound meaning behind his words. It wasn't until I embarked on the journey of adulthood that the true magnitude of this wisdom began to reveal itself.

I vividly remember a pivotal moment during my early twenties when I found myself in the midst of a heated argument with a close friend. We were both passionate about our viewpoints, and our voices grew louder and more forceful with each passing moment. It was as if we were engaged in a battle of words, each trying to overpower the other.

In the midst of this verbal chaos, my grandfather's words echoed in my mind. I realized that true communication is not about overpowering or silencing the other person; it's about creating a space for understanding and connection. With this newfound insight, I took a deep breath and made a conscious effort to listen. I let go of my need to be right and allowed my friend to express their thoughts without interruption. As I opened myself to truly hearing their perspective, a remarkable transformation occurred. The tension in the room dissipated, replaced by a sense of empathy and mutual respect. Our conversation shifted from a battle of egos to a genuine exchange of ideas. In that moment, I understood the power of active listening and the importance of giving others the space to be heard. Since that transformative experience, I have dedicated myself to mastering the art of effective communication. I have studied countless books, attended workshops, and engaged in conversations with people from all walks of life. Through these experiences, I have learned invaluable lessons that I can barely wait to share with you in this book.

So many of us, you see, know how to talk, but to listen is an entirely different thing. We want to be heard, but do we ourselves hear and listen to those who are speaking to us?

In a world dominated by noise and distractions, genuine conversations have become a rarity. We often find ourselves engrossed in our own thoughts, waiting for our turn to speak, rather than truly absorbing the essence of what others are trying to convey. But what if I told you that by mastering the art of listening, you could unlock a world of endless possibilities?

Welcome to the world of *How to Talk to Anyone,* a guidebook designed to revolutionize your conversational skills and transform the way you connect with people. Within these pages, we will unravel the secrets of effective communication and unveil the power of attentive listening. Imagine a world where every conversation becomes an opportunity for growth, understanding, and connection.

Through the magic of active listening, you will discover the hidden gems in the words of those around you. Their stories, experiences, and perspectives will enrich your own existence, allowing you to see the world through a kaleidoscope of diverse lenses. The ability to truly listen is a superpower that transcends boundaries. It is the key to forging meaningful relationships, fostering empathy, and resolving conflicts. Whether you are a shy introvert longing to break free from the shackles of social anxiety or an extroverted chatterbox craving more meaningful interactions, this book will equip you with the tools to navigate any conversation with finesse and authenticity. But this journey is not solely about others; it is about self-discovery. By immersing ourselves in the art of attentive listening, we uncover hidden aspects of our own personalities. We learn to cultivate patience, curiosity, and an insatiable thirst for knowledge.

As our ability to listen deepens, so does our capacity for personal growth and transformation. In these pages, you will find practical strategies, insightful anecdotes, and eye-opening research that will challenge your preconceived notions about communication. You will learn to navigate the treacherous waters of small talk, master the art of asking meaningful questions, and develop an unwavering presence that captivates and engages others. So, are you ready to embark on this transformative journey? Are you ready to transcend the barriers that block genuine connections? I know I am, and whether this book found you or you found it, I am grateful that paths have crossed. Let us embark on a quest to become exceptional listeners and elevate our conversations from mundane exchanges to profound exchanges of ideas, emotions, and dreams.

Get ready to unleash the power of conversation, to connect with anyone, anywhere, and to create lasting bonds that transcend the superficial. Join me as we embark on this adventure, where the art of listening becomes the catalyst for a richer, more fulfilling life. Let's go and discover the extraordinary world that awaits us on the other side of genuine, heartfelt conversations.

Chapter 1:

ABCs of Effective Communication

"A" is for awkward silences, and "Z," I guess we'll go for Zany misunderstandings.

I remember a couple of years ago, over Christmas break, I decided to head out home for the festive season. Mom, at that time, decided that she would make a spectacle out of her youngest coming home, but too late; she'd caught a bit of a bug the day just before Christmas Eve, leaving me, the beloved son, to go out and save the day.

First on the list was picking up some last-minute gifts from the local mall. As I entered the bustling shopping center, I was immediately greeted by a sea of frantic shoppers. Determined to find the perfect presents, I weaved through the crowd, only to find myself in a store that specialized in clown accessories. Awkwardly, I tried to explain that I was looking for something less comical, but the shopkeeper seemed convinced that a rubber chicken would be the ideal gift for my aunt. Needless to say, I swiftly made my exit, empty-handed and bewildered.

Next, I ventured into the grocery store to pick up some ingredients for our Christmas feast. Armed with a shopping list, I navigated the aisles, carefully selecting each item. However, in my haste, I misread *eggnog* as *eggplant*. Imagine my surprise when I arrived home with bags full of eggplants instead of the creamy holiday beverage. My mom's face turned from confusion to laughter as she realized the mix-up, and we spent the evening brainstorming creative uses for an abundance of eggplants. But the misadventures didn't end there. On my way back home, I encountered a man with a long white beard and a red suit. Assuming he was a festive mall Santa, I cheerfully exclaimed, "Ho ho ho!" To my embarrassment, it turned out he was just a fellow traveler with a penchant for holiday-themed attire. We exchanged awkward smiles and hurriedly went our separate ways. Through these humorous escapades, I learned that effective communication is not just about conveying messages clearly but also about embracing the unexpected and finding joy in the mishaps. As we learn about all the things that make effective communication what it is, may we remember to laugh, learn, and embrace the delightful chaos that comes with connecting with others.

What Is Meant by Effective Communication?

Effective communication—what exactly is meant by that? I mean, it is, after all, a term that is so widely thrown around nowadays in the world of business and, of course, the world of self-help.

Simply put, it refers to our ability to convey messages in a clear, compelling, and persuasive manner that fosters understanding and meaningful interaction between individuals or groups. In today's fast-paced and interconnected world, mastering effective communication skills has become more crucial than ever. And there's a whole science and formula to the first part, which is **the skill of being able to convey ideas concisely and precisely**. This involves organizing thoughts in a logical manner and using language that is easily understood by the target audience. In doing so, we can avoid any confusion or misunderstanding that might arise due to convoluted expressions or jargon.

In the final semester of college, the speaker, who was a charismatic gentleman, possessed an uncanny ability to transform even the simplest of ideas into something profound yet easily understandable. One particular analogy he used left a lasting impression on me. He began by introducing the analogy of a train. He explained that communication is like a train journey, with the message being the train itself. Just as a train needs a clear destination, our communication should have a specific goal or purpose. This analogy instantly captured my attention because it made the abstract concept of effective communication more relatable and tangible.

He then went on to explain that, just like a train needs a well-defined route, our communication should follow a logical and organized structure. By outlining the main points and supporting them with relevant examples, we ensure that our message is coherent and easy to follow. This analogy helped me understand the importance of structuring my own communication in a way that guides the listener along a clear path.

And I'm not yet done. Another thing that was emphasized was the significance of a train's engine—the core message that drives the entire journey. Similarly, our communication should have a strong and impactful central idea. By distilling complex concepts into a concise and memorable message, we can effectively convey our ideas and leave a lasting impression on our audience. The speaker's use of the train analogy made the topic of effective communication engaging and relatable. It is what helped me visualize the key elements of successful communication and provided a framework for me to apply in my own interactions. Remember that by having a clear destination, following a well-defined route, and ensuring a powerful engine, we can convey our ideas concisely and precisely. The speaker's use of the train analogy brought this concept to life, making it both compelling and memorable.

You might be reading this and thinking to yourself: How can I distill abstract concepts and make them more easily understandable? I've got a few tips for you:

- **Get to the Point**: Cut through the fluff and get straight to the heart of your message. Imagine you're texting a friend who's always in a hurry. Be concise and clear, and avoid unnecessary details. Remember, precision is key! two

- **Paint a Picture**: Descriptions make the biggest of differences. Bring your ideas to life by using vivid language and relatable examples. Think of it as telling a captivating story to a friend over a cup of coffee. By painting a picture with your words, you'll make your message more engaging and easier to understand.

Take a look at these two examples and think about which one would make you sit upright in your chair:

Example 1

The place was packed and full of people.

Example 2

The atmosphere was alive, and everyone's excitement was palpable; it clung to the room like a thick layer of peanut butter and jelly on a sandwich.

- **Embrace the Power of Analogies**: Just like our train analogy earlier, analogies can be powerful tools to convey complex ideas in a simple and relatable way. Compare your message to something familiar or use metaphors to make it easier for others to grasp your point.

- **Banish Jargon**: Avoid using technical jargon or industry-specific terms when communicating with a wider audience. Instead, opt for everyday language that everyone can understand. Remember, you want your message to resonate with as many people as possible.

- **Practice, Practice, Practice**: The more you practice conveying your ideas, the better you'll become at precision. Engage in conversations, give presentations, or even write blog posts to refine your communication skills. Confidence and clarity go hand in hand!

The second part of the mix is **active listening**, which is something that goes beyond simply hearing words but rather involves fully engaging with the speaker, understanding their perspective, and responding appropriately. Active listening not only helps to build rapport and trust, but it also allows for a deeper understanding of the message being conveyed. Nonverbal communication, such as body language and facial expressions, also plays a significant role in effective communication. These subtle cues can often convey emotions or intentions more powerfully than words alone. Being aware of your own nonverbal signals and interpreting those of others can enhance communication and prevent misinterpretation.

Nonverbal Communication: What Their Expressions Really Mean

- **Posture**

    - Upright posture: It conveys confidence, attentiveness, and openness.

    - Slouched posture: It suggests low energy, lack of confidence, or disinterest.

    - Leaning forward: By understanding interest, engagement, and active listening.

    - Crossed arms: Often signifies defensiveness, resistance, or a closed-off attitude.

    - Open arms and a relaxed stance: Indicates approachability and openness to communication.

    - Nodding: Shows agreement, understanding, or encouragement.

- **Facial Expressions**

    - Smile: This generally signifies happiness, friendliness, and approachability.

    - Raised eyebrows: Indicates surprise, curiosity, or interest.

    - Frowning: Suggests displeasure, concern, or disagreement.

    - Eye contact: Maintaining eye contact shows attentiveness, interest, and respect.

- Squinting: This can indicate skepticism, confusion, or concentration.

- Raised or furrowed forehead: May suggest confusion, concern, or deep thought.

- Yawning: Often signifies boredom, fatigue, or disinterest.

By understanding these cues, you can gain valuable insights into the speaker's emotions, attitudes, and intentions. By observing and understanding these cues, you can better connect with others, build rapport, and respond appropriately.

Nonverbal Communication: Showing That You Are a Confident Speaker

Confidence isn't about superiority. It is about owning who you are in your skin and expressing yourself as authentically as you can. Your body speaks to the way you carry yourself. Here's how you can show and convey that you are a confident speaker through the way you carry yourself:

- **Posture**

    - Upright and aligned posture: Stand tall with your shoulders back, conveying confidence and poise.

    - Balanced weight distribution: Distribute your weight evenly on both feet, showing stability and confidence.

    - Open body stance: Avoid crossing your arms or legs, keeping your body open and receptive to the audience.

- **Facial Expressions**

  - Eye contact: Maintain consistent eye contact with your audience to establish a connection and show confidence in your message.

  - Display a genuine smile when appropriate, as it conveys warmth, approachability, and confidence.

  - Avoid excessive tension or frowning, as it can convey nervousness or discomfort.

- **Gestures**

  - Purposeful hand movements: Use deliberate and controlled gestures to emphasize key points, displaying confidence and conviction.

  - Open palm gestures: Show your palms occasionally, as it signals openness, honesty, and confidence.

  - Smooth and natural gestures: Avoid fidgeting or excessive movements, as it can indicate nervousness or a lack of confidence.

- **Voice**

  - Clear and steady voice: Speak with clarity, projecting your voice confidently, and maintaining a steady pace.

  - Use appropriate variations in tone to emphasize important points and maintain audience engagement.

  - Speak at a moderate pace, allowing your words to be easily understood and conveying confidence in your message.

It's also the ability to adapt communication styles to different situations and audiences.

Imagine you're at a party, surrounded by a diverse group of people. You crack a joke, expecting laughter and applause. But wait! The response is a mix of confusion, polite smiles, and uproarious laughter. What just happened? Well, that's what happens when you throw diversity into the mix of effective communication.

Now, let's imagine a hypothetical scenario where you're trying to organize a surprise birthday party for your friend, and you need to communicate with three different people: Sarah, a direct and straightforward person; Raj, a reserved and indirect person; and Maria, an expressive and emotional person.

When you approach Sarah, you might say, "Hey, we're throwing a surprise party for John. Can you help us out?" Sarah, being direct, would appreciate the straightforwardness and respond with, "Sure, count me in!"

Next, you approach Raj and say, "Hey, I heard John's birthday is coming up. It would be great if we could do something special for him." Raj, being reserved and indirect, might respond with a hesitant, "Hmm, I'll think about it," leaving you unsure if he's on board or not.

Finally, you approach Maria and excitedly exclaim, "Oh my gosh, we're throwing the most amazing surprise party for John! It's going to be epic!" Maria, being expressive and emotional, would mirror your enthusiasm and respond with, "Oh wow, that sounds incredible! I'm in, and I'll bring the confetti cannons!"

In this example, despite conveying the same message, each person interprets it differently based on their communication style and background. Sarah appreciates directness, Raj prefers subtlety, and Maria thrives on emotion and excitement.

So, you see, our diverse backgrounds shape our communication styles, and understanding these differences allows us to adapt and connect with others more effectively. It's like learning a secret language that unlocks the beauty and reduces the frustration of human interaction. When you tailor your communication to meet someone's needs, it essentially means that you recognize and understand their cultural differences, individual preferences, and varying needs. By tailoring the message to specific contexts, we can maximize the impact and relevance of their communication.

Here are also a few common misunderstandings that can occur due to different communication styles:

- **Direct vs. Indirect**: People with direct communication styles may perceive those with indirect styles as being unclear or evasive, while those with indirect styles may see direct communicators as rude or aggressive.

- **High Context vs. Low Context**: In high-context cultures, where much meaning is conveyed through nonverbal cues and context, people from low-context cultures may miss subtle messages and interpret things too literally, leading to misunderstandings.

- **Verbal vs. Nonverbal**: Some individuals rely heavily on verbal communication, while others place more emphasis on nonverbal cues. Misunderstandings can arise when one person misses or misinterprets nonverbal signals, such as body language or facial expressions.

- **Formal vs. Informal**: Different cultures and individuals have varying levels of formality in their communication. Using overly formal language with someone who prefers a more casual approach can create confusion or make them feel distant, while being too informal with someone who values formality may be seen as disrespectful.

- **Emotional Expression**: People have different comfort levels when it comes to expressing emotions. Misunderstandings can occur when someone interprets a lack of emotional expression as indifference or when someone perceives emotional expression as excessive or dramatic.

Lastly, beyond the technical aspects, effective communication is also about *fostering a genuine connection and establishing a rapport with others*. It involves being empathetic, understanding, and compassionate towards others' perspectives and feelings. When we create a safe and inclusive environment, that encourages open dialogue and collaboration, which often leads to better receptivity toward what we are trying to share.

Are Communication Skills Necessary for Speaking to Anyone?

Communication skills are necessary for all, regardless of profession or the dynamic in our personal lives. In fact, having strong communication skills is one of the most important qualities that one can possess.

My grandfather used to tell me this story about an old colleague of his named Jerry. "He was not a smart book fella, but boy was he charismatic and charming—the kind of man who could sell snow to an Eskimo," he used to say. It just goes to show that sometimes it's not about what you know, but how you convey it. Being able to share your ideas and thoughts is a powerful tool that can take you far in life. Whether it's in a professional setting or in personal relationships, having strong communication skills can make all the difference.

One of the areas in the workplace where, whether you are working in a team or independently, being able to communicate effectively with your colleagues, clients, and superiors can make all the difference in achieving your goals. Good communication can help you build relationships, gain trust, and resolve conflicts. I mean, think about it: You don't want to be the kind of co-worker who has everyone walking all over them, and neither do you want to be the one who steps on toes left, right, and center, as well as offends everyone. You want to be able to stand up for yourself while still managing to treat others with dignity and respect.

In addition to the professional benefits, strong communication skills can also greatly enhance your personal life. There are so many platonic and romantic relationships that drift away because of a lack of communication. When you don't communicate with your people, you begin to make assumptions, and assumptions are what typically lead to unmet needs. Sure, there is that momentary discomfort that comes from having honest conversations, but the rewards are worth the while. I mean, think about it: Better boundaries and reciprocity are things that everyone deserves to have and experience in their relationships.

So, whether you are interacting with friends, family, or romantic partners, being able to align the words that are coming out of your mouth with the desires that reside in your heart will lead to better fulfillment and contentment.

What Impact Does Effective Communication Have on Others?

It's not always easy to be honest with people, especially when you know that what you have to say might not be well-received. But here's the thing: being honest is one of the most important things you can do for yourself and for those around you. When you're honest, you're showing people that you respect them enough to tell them the truth, even if it's something they might not want to hear. And while they might not always like what you have to say, they will always respect you for being honest.

But here's the other thing: How you communicate that honesty is just as important as the honesty itself. Everyone deserves to be communicated with in a way that helps them maintain their sense of dignity. That means communicating with respect and dignity and making sure that everyone feels seen and heard. When you communicate in this way, you're not just doing it for yourself but for those around you as well.

How do you feel when someone communicates with you in a way that makes you feel small, powerless, or simply insignificant? It doesn't feel good, right? It makes you feel... naked. And it's not just about how you feel; it's also about how that communication affects your relationships with the people around you. You're more likely to continue interacting with someone whose presence doesn't make you feel threatened but someone who talks to you like you're nothing. It's pretty obvious that you might want to create as much distance between them as possible.

Be honest, but be kind. Communicate with respect and dignity, and remember that everyone deserves to be seen and heard. When you do these things, you'll not only be shaping yourself into the kind of speaker that is remembered, but you'll also be making the world a better place for everyone around you.

And lastly, remember that the hallmark of healthy and effective communication isn't so much about what you say but so much about how you say it. It's about your body language and your overall delivery. By focusing more on how we communicate, we can create an environment that fosters open dialogue, mutual respect, and healthier relationship dynamics.

Chapter 2:

Learn the Art of Public Speaking

My English teacher in the 8th grade was a powerhouse of a woman. She was a gifted speaker, a force to be reckoned with. We all called her a half-woman, half-mythical creature because when she delivered a lesson on Shakespeare or anything at all, even those who didn't care much about their language would sit up straight and hang on to her every word.

Her presence commanded attention, effortlessly filling the room with passion and knowledge. It was as if she possessed a magical ability to captivate even the most disinterested minds, leaving us spellbound and hungry for more. The way she spoke, with conviction and eloquence, made us believe in the power of words. She had a way of breathing life into the driest of subjects, making them come alive before our very eyes.

Every lesson was a performance, a theatrical masterpiece. She would stride across the room, her voice resonating with confidence as if she owned the stage. Her gestures were purposeful, her expressions were animated, and her eyes sparkled with enthusiasm. It was impossible not to be drawn into her world, a world where words had the power to inspire, educate, and transform. But it wasn't just her delivery that made her an exceptional public speaker. It was her genuine passion for the subject matter. She believed in the importance of effective communication and instilled in us the desire to master this art form. She taught us that public speaking was not just about standing in front of a crowd and delivering a speech but about connecting with people on a deeper level. She encouraged us to find our own unique voice, to embrace our individuality, and to use our words to make a difference. She taught us the power of storytelling, the art of persuasion, and the importance of body language. She pushed us out of our comfort zones, challenging us to speak up, to share our thoughts and ideas, and to overcome our fears. Little did we know that those early lessons would shape our lives and empower us to confidently speak to anyone, anywhere, at any time.

The skills we learned in that classroom transcended the boundaries of academia. They became life skills and tools that would serve us well in every aspect of our personal and professional lives. Looking back, I realize how fortunate we were to have had such an extraordinary teacher. She not only taught us the mechanics of public speaking but also instilled in us the belief that our voices mattered. She showed us that with the right words, delivered with passion and purpose, we could move mountains and inspire change.

Basic Principles of Public Speaking

Not everyone is born a public speaker, but we can all learn how to become one. The ability to confidently address a crowd, deliver a compelling message, and leave a lasting impact is not reserved for a select few. It is a skill that can be cultivated and honed through the understanding and application of basic principles of public speaking. In this section, we will delve into these fundamental principles, equipping you with the tools and knowledge necessary to transform yourself into the kind of speaker who leaves their audience hanging on your every word.

Start With a Plan

When it comes to public speaking, starting with a plan is as important as the very air that we breathe. Just like a skilled architect meticulously designs a blueprint before constructing a building, a successful speaker carefully crafts a plan before stepping onto the stage. Your plan serves as the foundation for your speech, providing structure, coherence, and clarity. When starting with a plan, you lay the groundwork for a well-organized and impactful presentation.

So, where do you start with this plan of yours? By defining your objective, what do you want to achieve with your speech? Is it to inform, persuade, entertain, or inspire? Once you have a clear objective in mind, outline the main points that support your goal. These main points will act as the pillars of your speech, guiding your audience through a logical and cohesive flow of ideas.

Next, consider the needs and interests of your audience as you develop your plan. What information or insights would resonate with them? How can you capture their attention and keep them engaged? Tailor your content to meet their expectations and address their concerns. Remember, a well-planned speech is not just about what you want to say but also about what your audience needs to hear.

Also, think about the overall structure of your speech. A strong introduction sets the stage, grabs attention, and establishes a connection with your audience. The body of your speech should go into the main points, providing supporting evidence, examples, and anecdotes.

Last but not least, and the cherry on top, think about a memorable conclusion that wraps up your key ideas, leaving a lasting impression on your listeners. Starting with a plan not only helps you stay focused and organized but also helps establish you as credible. If you're going to be delivering a speech on productivity, do you think the audience will want to listen to someone who doesn't seem to have their ducks in a row? probably not. Knowing that you have a well-thought-out roadmap to guide you gives you the assurance and peace of mind to deliver your message effectively. So, before you step out onto the stage, take the time to build something that will serve as your compass, ensuring that you navigate those moments up on stage with purpose, clarity, and impact.

Broaden Your Perception

As speakers, it is easy to fall into the trap of focusing solely on our own perspective and assumptions but to truly connect with our audience and deliver a compelling message; we must expand our horizons and embrace a broader understanding of the world and culture around us.

Broadening your perception involves stepping outside of your comfort zone and actively seeking diverse perspectives. Take the time to research and explore different viewpoints, cultures, and experiences. This not only enriches your own knowledge but also allows you to connect with a wider range of audience members. When you do this, you gain a deeper appreciation for the diversity of your audience. You become more attuned to their needs, interests, and values. This understanding enables you to tailor your message in a way that resonates with a broader range of individuals, fostering inclusivity and engagement.

It is something that can potentially open the door to fresh ideas and innovative approaches. It encourages you to think beyond the confines of your own experiences and tap into the collective wisdom of humanity. This newfound perspective can infuse your speeches with creativity, originality, and relevance. Embracing a broader perception also helps you anticipate and address potential objections or concerns that your audience may have. By understanding different viewpoints, you can proactively acknowledge and respond to differing opinions, fostering a sense of respect and open dialogue.

Work on Your Preparation

Working on your preparedness is a key principle that can make a world of difference in your public speaking endeavors. Picture this: you're standing in front of a crowd, ready to deliver your speech. Suddenly, you realize you forgot your notes; your mind goes blank, and panic sets in. We've all had nightmares like this, haven't we?

To avoid such nightmares becoming a reality, you have to prioritize preparedness. Being well-prepared not only boosts your confidence but also ensures a smooth and successful delivery. So, how can you work on your preparedness?

First and foremost, *familiarize yourself with your topic.* Research, read, and gather information to become an expert on the subject matter. The more you know, the more confident you'll feel when addressing your audience. Plus, being well-informed allows you to answer questions with ease and authority.

Next, *organize your thoughts and structure your speech.* Create an outline or a script that outlines the key points you want to cover. This will help maintain a logical flow and prevent you from getting lost in a sea of words. Remember, a well-structured speech is like a well-constructed building—it stands strong and leaves a lasting impression.

Now, *sprinkle in a dash of humor.* They say laughter is the best medicine, and it certainly holds true in public speaking. Incorporating light-hearted humor can help you connect with your audience, break the ice, and create a relaxed atmosphere. But you have to strike a balance. Avoid excessive jokes or inappropriate humor that may detract from your message. Keep it light, relevant, and in good taste.

Practice, practice, and practice some more. Rehearse your speech multiple times, either in front of a mirror or with a trusted friend or family member. Pay attention to your tone, gestures, and timing. This will help you refine your delivery and ensure a polished performance.

Lastly, *expect the unexpected.* Murphy's Law states that anything that can go wrong will go wrong. Technical glitches, distractions, or unexpected questions may arise. By preparing for these potential pitfalls, you can handle them with grace and composure. Remember, even the most seasoned speakers get hiccups along the way. It's how you handle them that sets you apart.

Focus on Presentation

Presentation matters if you want your audience to be hanging on your very last word. Imagine being in a room where the speaker rambles on, jumping from one topic to another without a clear direction. It would be easy to lose interest and disengage, correct? That's why a focused presentation is crucial for delivering a powerful message.

To create a focused presentation, start by refining and defining the essence of your message. What is the main idea or takeaway you want your audience to remember? Once you have identified your core message, structure your speech around it. Every point you make, every story you share, and every piece of evidence you present should support and reinforce your core message.

The next part is clarity. Be clear and concise in your delivery. Avoid using jargon or complex language that may potentially confuse your audience. Simple works best in most cases. Strive for reliability. Use examples that your audience would be able to easily identify with. For example, if you are giving a talk on productivity hacks and procrastination and want to share an anecdote with your audience, you could use something like: Imagine you have a deadline looming for an important project, but instead of diving into the work, you find yourself scrolling through social media, watching funny cat videos, and suddenly realizing hours have slipped away. We've all been there, right? That feeling of frustration and regret as we realize we've wasted precious time.

Don't forget about the power of storytelling. Stories have a unique ability to captivate an audience and make your message memorable. Incorporate relevant anecdotes, personal experiences, or case studies that align with your core message. This will not only add depth and authenticity to your presentation but also help your audience connect with your message on an emotional level.

The body says things that the voice does not express; pay attention to your body language and vocal delivery. Maintain eye contact with your audience, use gestures to emphasize key points, and vary your tone and pace to keep your listeners engaged. A focused presentation is not just about the words you say but also how you deliver them.

Lastly, be mindful of time management. Respect your audience's time by staying within the allocated timeframe. I know that it can be so easy to get carried away, so make sure you practice and time yourself during rehearsals so that you have enough time to go through everything that you need to go through.

Rate Your Performance

Self-evaluation is a powerful tool when it comes to public speaking. It involves stepping back, reflecting on your strengths and areas for improvement, and honestly assessing your own delivery. It is how we can gain valuable insights and make meaningful adjustments to enhance our speaking skills.

Things that you can think about include: What are the qualities that make you an effective speaker? Perhaps you have a natural ability to connect with your audience, or you excel at storytelling. Recognizing and acknowledging your strengths allows you to leverage them and build upon them in future presentations. It also boosts your confidence as you become aware of the unique qualities that set you apart as a speaker.

On the other hand, it is also about identifying areas for improvement. Are there aspects of your delivery that could be refined or polished? Maybe you tend to speak too quickly, or you struggle with maintaining eye contact. By honestly assessing these areas, you can develop a plan to address them. Seek feedback from trusted individuals, record and review your speeches, and actively work on improving these aspects through practice and self-awareness.

Self-evaluation also extends beyond the technical aspects of speaking. It involves reflecting on the impact and effectiveness of your message. Did your speech resonate with your audience? Did you achieve your intended goals? Evaluating the reception and impact of your message allows you to fine-tune your content and delivery to better connect with your listeners.

You must, however, also approach self-evaluation with a balanced mindset. While it's important to identify areas for improvement, it's equally important to celebrate the successes we achieve. Recognize the progress you've made and the milestones you've achieved. By acknowledging your growth, you can maintain a positive outlook and continue to strive for excellence.

Make It Personalized

When you connect with your listeners on a personal level, you create a sense of relatability and empathy, which are two very important ingredients needed to build stronger connections and engagement. So, how can you make your presentation more personalized?

Understand your audience. Research and gather insights about their demographics, interests, and needs. This knowledge allows you to tailor your content and examples to their specific context, making them more relevant and relatable. When you speak directly to their experiences and challenges, you demonstrate that you understand their perspective and are there to provide valuable insights.

Share personal stories and experiences. Open up and let your audience get a glimpse into your own journey or struggles related to the topic at hand. By sharing your vulnerabilities and triumphs, you create a sense of authenticity and trust. This vulnerability can inspire and motivate your audience, showing them that they are not alone in their experiences.

Human psychology is quite fascinating, and there's a reason why these personalization tactics work. We have an innate desire to feel understood and connected. So, when your presentation is personalized, you tap into this fundamental need, creating a powerful emotional connection. This connection enhances the overall impact of your message, as your audience feels seen, heard, and validated. Personalization also helps to overcome the barrier of information overload. In today's fast-paced world, we are bombarded with an overwhelming amount of information. By making your presentation personalized, you cut through the noise and capture your audience's attention. When they see themselves reflected in your examples and stories, they are more likely to engage with and retain the information you're sharing.

Exhibit Your Passion

Exhibiting passion is like setting off fireworks on stage; it ignites the atmosphere, captivates your audience, and leaves a lasting impression. Picture this: you step onto the stage, your eyes shining with enthusiasm, your voice brimming with energy, and your body language radiating excitement. Your passion becomes contagious, spreading like wildfire among your listeners. They lean in, eager to absorb every word, every gesture, and every ounce of your infectious zeal.

Passion is the secret ingredient that transforms a good presentation into an unforgettable experience. It's the fuel that propels your words, infusing them with intensity and conviction. When you exhibit passion, you become a magnetic force, drawing your audience into your world, and inspiring them to embrace your message.

But how do you exhibit passion? It starts with finding your spark—that deep-rooted enthusiasm for your topic. Discover what truly excites you—what makes your heart race and your eyes light up. Whether it's a cause you're passionate about, a subject you've dedicated years to studying, or a personal experience that has shaped your perspective, let that passion shine through in your words and actions. Share personal anecdotes, use vivid language, and express genuine emotion to connect with your audience on a deeper level. Be confident in your knowledge and expertise, and let your enthusiasm be contagious. Remember, passion is not just about what you say but also how you say it. Use your body language, gestures, and tone of voice to convey your excitement and engage your listeners. Lastly, remember that passion is all about authenticity. When you're speaking from a genuine place, your audience will feel that.

Don't Aim for Perfection

Perfection is the enemy of progress; let's just say it's the enemy of anything at all.

Perfection is not the ultimate goal. You want to inspire, inform, and make an impact. Striving for perfection will only create unnecessary pressure and hinder your ability to connect with your audience authentically. Instead, focus on delivering a genuine and impactful message. Here's why:

Firstly, aiming for perfection often leads to self-imposed stress and anxiety. The fear of making mistakes or not meeting unrealistic expectations can overshadow your ability to communicate effectively. Embrace the idea that imperfections are a natural part of the speaking process. It's through these imperfections that your personality shines through, making you relatable and approachable to your audience.

Perfection is also subjective. What may seem perfect to one person may not resonate with another. Instead of fixating on flawless delivery, prioritize the content and the connection you establish with your audience. Focus on delivering value, sharing insights, and inspiring your listeners. Authenticity and genuine engagement will leave a lasting impact far greater than striving for an unattainable standard of perfection.

You also don't want to stifle your creativity and spontaneity, and what perfectionism will do is restrict you from adapting to the energy and dynamics of the audience. Embrace the fluidity of public speaking, allowing room for improvisation and genuine moments of connection. Remember, it's the human element that makes a speech memorable, not flawless execution.

Lastly, by letting go of the need for perfection, you open yourself up to growth and learning. Embrace constructive feedback and use it as an opportunity to refine your skills. Recognize that every speaking engagement is a chance to improve and evolve as a speaker. Embrace the journey rather than fixating on an unattainable destination.

There really is a speaker within each of us that is waiting to be unleashed. Sure, for some of us, it's going to take a lot more work than most, but if you believe in yourself greatly enough, anything is possible. Deep down, we all possess the potential to become powerful and impactful speakers. It may require stepping out of our comfort zones, honing our skills, and embracing continuous growth, but the journey is worth it.

Believing in yourself is the first step towards unlocking your speaking potential. It's about recognizing that you have a unique voice and perspective that deserves to be heard. Embrace the idea that your words have the power to inspire, educate, and influence others. Trust in your abilities and have faith in your capacity to grow and improve.

While some individuals may have a natural inclination towards public speaking, it doesn't mean that those who initially struggle cannot excel. With dedication, practice, and a willingness to learn, you can overcome any obstacles that stand in your way.

Chapter 3:

Different Modes of Public

Speaking

Have you ever marveled at the diverse strategies employed by skilled orators? Just like masterful tacticians on the battlefield, public speakers possess a range of techniques at their disposal, each akin to a unique weapon in their arsenal. These modes of public speaking allow them to adapt, connect, and leave a lasting impact on their audience.

Think of a seasoned speaker as a versatile strategist adept at selecting the right weapon for every speaking engagement. They may wield the precision of an analytical speaker, presenting facts and data with razor-sharp clarity. Alternatively, they might harness the power of storytelling, weaving narratives that captivate and resonate with their listeners.

But the true mastery lies in the art of combining these modes, creating a symphony of persuasion and influence. Like a conductor leading an orchestra, skilled speakers blend the informative and the entertaining, the analytical and the emotional, to craft a compelling and unforgettable experience for their audience.

In this chapter, we delve into the captivating world of public speaking modes. We unravel the secrets behind each technique, exploring when and how to employ them effectively. Ready? Let's get going!

Manuscript Mode

Imagine a skilled architect meticulously crafting a blueprint before constructing a magnificent building. In the realm of public speaking, the manuscript mode is the same as that blueprint—a methodical approach that involves writing and delivering a speech verbatim from a carefully prepared script.

In manuscript mode, every word is chosen meticulously, and every sentence is thoughtfully crafted. This model is characterized by its precision and deliberation, leaving no room for improvisation or spontaneous deviations. It is a mode favored by those who seek to ensure utmost accuracy and control over their message.

Here are some examples of scenarios where the manuscript mode would be used:

- **Formal Ceremonies**: Formal ceremonies such as graduation speeches, award presentations, or inaugural addresses require speakers to rely on a carefully prepared script to ensure that their words are delivered precisely and with the desired impact. Manuscript mode allows speakers to convey important messages with clarity and maintain a sense of formality and professionalism.

- **Legal Proceedings**: In courtrooms or legal proceedings, this mode is used by attorneys when presenting their arguments or delivering opening and closing statements. The precise language and structure of a prepared script help lawyers present their cases accurately and persuasively. If they follow a script, they can ensure that no critical points are missed and that their arguments are delivered with precision.

- **Scientific Conferences**. Speakers in this context often rely on a written script to accurately communicate complex scientific concepts and data. The script allows them to present their research with clarity, ensuring that the audience understands the nuances of their work.

In each of these scenarios, we can see how the speakers rely on a prepared script; this allows them to navigate these situations with confidence and ensure that their words have the desired impact. It also helps them maintain professionalism and effectively communicate complex information.

Advantages

- You are given the ability to deliver information with precision and accuracy. By following a prepared script, you can ensure that every word and detail is conveyed exactly as intended. Which is particularly valuable in situations where accuracy is necessary, such as in legal proceedings or scientific presentations.

- It also allows you to refine your language, structure your arguments, and create a polished delivery. With the luxury of time for careful crafting, you can use sophisticated vocabulary, employ rhetorical devices, and ensure that your speech flows seamlessly. This can enhance the overall impact of the message and leave a lasting impression on the audience.

Disadvantages

- There's a lack of spontaneity: Since the speech is delivered verbatim from a script, there is limited room for improvisation or adapting to the immediate audience's response. This can make the speech feel rehearsed and less engaging for the listeners.

- It limits the connection with the audience: Manuscript mode can sometimes mess with your ability to connect with the audience. When speakers are solely focused on reading from the script, they may struggle to establish eye contact, engage with gestures, or maintain a natural flow of conversation. This can create a barrier between the speaker and the audience, making it harder to establish a genuine connection.

- There is also the added risk of over-reliance on the script. You may become too dependent on the written words, leading to a lack of flexibility or adaptability during the speech. This can make it challenging to respond to unexpected situations or adjust the delivery based on the audience's reactions.

While manuscript mode offers you precision and control over your message, you will need to actively work to overcome the potential drawbacks. You can do this by incorporating gestures, maintaining eye contact, and infusing the delivery with passion and authenticity.

Impromptu Mode

Imagine being handed a microphone and asked to speak on a topic without any preparation. Welcome to the world of impromptu mode, where you have to rely on your wit, spontaneity, and quick thinking to deliver a speech on the spot. This mode is like a thrilling tightrope walk, where you have to navigate uncharted territory with confidence and charm.

In impromptu mode, you are presented with a topic or question and must respond immediately without the luxury of a prepared script. This mode is characterized by its spontaneity and authenticity because it allows you to share your thoughts and ideas in real time, often drawing from your knowledge and personal experiences.

Impromptu mode can be used in various scenarios, such as:

- **Panel Discussions**: In panel discussions or Q&A sessions, impromptu mode shines. Speakers are called upon to provide insightful and spontaneous responses to questions from the audience or fellow panelists. This mode allows for dynamic and interactive conversations, fostering engaging discussions and diverse perspectives.

- **Toasts and Speeches**: Impromptu mode can be employed during toasts or short speeches at social events. When called upon to say a few words, speakers can rely on their ability to think on their feet and deliver heartfelt and off-the-cuff remarks. This mode adds a personal touch and a sense of authenticity to the occasion.

- **Job Interviews**: Impromptu mode is often put to the test during job interviews, where candidates may be asked unexpected questions or given impromptu tasks. This mode allows candidates to showcase their ability to think critically, communicate effectively, and demonstrate their knowledge and skills in real-time.

Advantages

One of the key advantages of impromptu mode is the opportunity to showcase quick-thinking skills. You must think on your feet, process information rapidly, and deliver coherent responses in real-time. This mode allows you to demonstrate your ability to handle unexpected situations with grace and confidence.

It also gives you a platform to express your genuine thoughts and ideas. Without the constraints of a prepared script, you can tap into your authentic voice, sharing insights and perspectives in a natural and unfiltered way. This authenticity is a solid foundation for building connections with your audience and fostering engagement and trust.

It also allows you to adapt to different speaking situations and audiences. Whether it's a panel discussion, a social gathering, or a job interview, you can tailor your responses to the specific context and audience. This adaptability showcases versatility and the ability to connect with diverse individuals.

Disadvantages

The main challenge of impromptu mode is the absence of preparation time. Speakers do not have the luxury of researching or organizing their thoughts in advance. This can make it challenging to deliver well-structured and comprehensive responses, particularly for complex or unfamiliar topics.

Without the guidance of a prepared script, there is a risk of delivering disjointed or incoherent responses. You may struggle to articulate your ideas effectively or may veer off-topic. It requires skill and practice to maintain clarity and coherence while thinking on your feet.

On-the-spot speaking can induce pressure and nervousness because you must perform without the safety net of a script. The spontaneous nature of impromptu mode can be intimidating, leading to anxiety or stage fright. But, with practice and confidence-building techniques, speakers can overcome these challenges.

Remember, practice and preparation in other speaking modes can also enhance impromptu skills, as a strong foundation of knowledge and communication techniques can support confident and coherent responses even in spontaneous situations.

Memorized Mode

Imagine stepping onto a stage with every word of your speech etched in your memory like a well-rehearsed play. Well, this is, so to speak, what memorized mode is. It is when you, as the speaker, deliver your message with unwavering precision and flawless recitation. It is much like a choreographed dance, where every movement and word are meticulously planned and executed.

In memorized mode, you commit your entire speech to memory, word for word. This approach allows for a seamless and polished delivery because you can maintain eye contact, engage with gestures, and establish a strong connection with your audience.

Memorized mode is commonly used in theatrical performances, such as plays, musicals, or monologues. Actors spend extensive time memorizing their lines to deliver a seamless and captivating performance. By committing the script to memory, they can fully embody their characters, maintain the flow of the story, and engage the audience with their flawless delivery.

They can also be used in high-profile keynote speeches at conferences or events. Speakers who have a well-rehearsed and memorized speech can deliver it with confidence and precision. This mode allows them to maintain a consistent and impactful delivery, ensuring that their key messages are conveyed effectively to inspire and motivate the audience.

Lastly, memorized mode is also often used in commemorative events, such as memorial services, anniversary celebrations, or historical reenactments. Speakers who have memorized their speeches can pay tribute, honor significant moments, or bring historical events to life with eloquence and authenticity.

Advantages

Flawless delivery: One of the key advantages of memorized mode is that it gives you the ability to deliver a speech with a flawless and polished delivery. By committing the script to memory, speakers can maintain a consistent pace, tone, and emphasis, ensuring that their message is conveyed exactly as intended. This can enhance the impact and effectiveness of the speech.

Increased Confidence: Memorizing a speech can boost your confidence. With the script firmly ingrained in your memory, you can focus more on engaging with the audience, maintaining eye contact, and using gestures effectively.

Disadvantages

Memorized mode can sometimes lead to rigidity in delivery. Since the speech is committed to memory, there is limited room for improvisation or adapting to the immediate audience response. This rigidity can make the speech feel rehearsed and less authentic, potentially hindering the speaker's ability to connect with the audience.

Memorizing a speech (or anything really) comes with the risk of memory lapses or forgetting a portion of the script. This can be particularly challenging if you become flustered or lose your train of thought. Recovering from a memory lapse in a memorized speech requires quick thinking and the ability to seamlessly continue without losing the audience's attention.

Memorized mode may limit your ability to adapt to unexpected circumstances or changes in the speaking environment. If the situation calls for adjustments or improvisation, speakers who rely solely on memorization may struggle to deviate from their prepared script. This lack of adaptability can make it difficult to respond to audience reactions or engage in spontaneous interactions.

Extemporaneous Mode

Extemporaneous mode is akin to artful balance—a dynamic approach that combines preparedness with spontaneity. This mode allows you to deliver a speech with a well-structured framework while incorporating improvisation and audience interaction. Extemporaneous mode is commonly used in various scenarios where flexibility and adaptability are key, for example:

- **Business Presentations**: In the corporate world, extemporaneous mode shines during business presentations. Speakers can prepare an outline or key points in advance, allowing them to maintain a structured flow. But they also have the freedom to adapt their delivery based on audience reactions, engage in impromptu discussions, and respond to questions in real-time. This mode showcases professionalism, expertise, and the ability to connect with stakeholders.

- **Panel Discussions**: Extemporaneous mode is also highly effective in panel discussions where multiple speakers share their insights on a particular topic. Each panelist can prepare their key points beforehand, ensuring a cohesive discussion. However, the true magic lies in the spontaneous interaction between panelists as they respond to each other's ideas, build upon them, and engage in lively exchanges. This mode fosters collaboration, diverse perspectives, and a dynamic exchange of knowledge.

- **Educational Settings**: Teachers also often use extemporaneous mode during classroom lectures or academic presentations. They can prepare the main content and structure in advance, ensuring a well-organized delivery. On the other hand, they can also adapt their approach based on students' responses, address questions on the spot, and create a more interactive and engaging learning environment. This mode promotes student engagement, critical thinking, and a personalized learning experience.

In each of these scenarios, we can see how the mode allows speakers to strike a balance between preparedness and spontaneity by combining a solid foundation of knowledge and a flexible delivery style.

Advantages

One of the key advantages of extemporaneous mode is the ability to adapt to the speaking situation and audience in real time. You can adjust your delivery, language, and examples based on the immediate feedback and engagement from the listeners. This flexibility allows for a more personalized and relevant speech, fostering audience connection and engagement.

This mode also allows you to deliver your message in a natural and authentic manner. While having a prepared outline or key points, you have the freedom to use your own words, tone, and style of delivery. This authenticity helps to establish trust, credibility, and a genuine connection with the audience.

The extemporaneous mode encourages speaker-audience interaction and engagement. You can actively involve the audience through questions, discussions, and incorporating their perspectives into the speech. This interactive approach creates a more dynamic and participatory speaking experience, fostering a sense of involvement and shared learning.

Disadvantages

- **Potential for Incoherence or Rambling**: Without the structure of a prepared script, there is a risk of delivering incoherent or rambling speeches. You may struggle to organize your thoughts on the spot, leading to disjointed or unclear messages. It requires practice and skill to maintain coherence and clarity while speaking extemporaneously.

- **Lack of Precision and Accuracy**: Extemporaneous mode may lead to a lack of precision and accuracy in delivering complex or technical information. Without the benefit of a prepared script, speakers may inadvertently omit important details or inaccurately convey information. This can be a challenge in fields that require precise and accurate communication, such as science or finance.

- **Increased Pressure and Nervousness**: Speaking extemporaneously can induce additional pressure and nervousness compared to other modes. The lack of a script or complete reliance on memory can heighten anxiety and stage fright. Speakers must manage their nerves effectively to ensure a confident and composed delivery.

Chapter 4:

Traits to Become a Great Public

Speaker

Imagine a room filled with eager faces hanging onto your every word. Your voice resonates with confidence, your gestures command attention, and your message leaves a lasting impact. What does it take to become a great public speaker? It's not just about having a way with words or a charismatic presence. It's about possessing a unique set of traits that captivate, inspire, and connect with your audience on a profound level. In this chapter, we will explore the essential qualities that pave the path to becoming a remarkable speaker. From mastering the art of storytelling to harnessing the power of body language, we will delve into the traits that can transform an ordinary presentation into an extraordinary experience. Whether you're a seasoned or aspiring speaker, there's something for all of you: All the secrets behind captivating an audience, leaving them spellbound, and making your mark as a truly exceptional public speaker.

Confidence to Face the Public

My grandfather, a man of few words but immense wisdom, would often share nuggets of insight that resonated deeply within me. One particular piece of advice has remained etched in my mind, guiding me through countless nerve-wracking moments. He would say, "If you're walking into a room for the very first time and you're nervous, you still have to walk in there like you know exactly who sent you there."

Those words, simple yet profound, became my mantra as I embarked on my journey to become a great public speaker. The power of confidence, I soon discovered, was not merely a facade to be worn but a force that emanated from within. It was the unwavering belief in oneself, the unshakable conviction that every word spoken held value and purpose.

As I stood before my first audience, my heart pounding in my chest, I summoned the strength to embody my grandfather's wisdom. With each step I took towards that podium, I felt a surge of energy coursing through my veins. I straightened my posture, lifted my chin, and met the gaze of those before me. In that moment, I realized that confidence was not about suppressing fear but rather embracing it and transforming it into a driving force.

The room fell silent as I began to speak, my voice steady and unwavering. The nervousness that once threatened to consume me now fueled my passion, propelling me forward. I shared my thoughts, my ideas, and my stories, connecting with the audience in a way I had never imagined possible. The power of confidence had unlocked a door within me, allowing me to step into my true potential as a speaker.

From that day forward, I carried my grandfather's wisdom with me, a constant reminder that confidence is not an external validation but a deep-rooted belief in one's abilities. It is the audacity to embrace vulnerability, to stand tall in the face of uncertainty, and to trust that the message within you is worthy of being heard.

Confidence is not about arrogance, self-righteousness, or thinking that you are better than the rest. It is a state of being that transcends ego and taps into the core of your authenticity. True confidence is rooted in a deep, unwavering belief in what you have to say and the value it holds for your audience.

As a speaker, confidence starts with a solid foundation of knowledge and preparation. It is the result of countless hours spent researching, crafting your message, and honing your delivery. When you have done the work and immersed yourself in the subject matter, you can stand before your audience with the assurance that you are well-equipped to share your insights.

But confidence is not just about what you know; it is also about how you communicate that knowledge. It is about the way you carry yourself on stage, the clarity and conviction in your voice, and the connection you establish with your audience. Here are a few keyways to exhibit confidence as a speaker:

- **Body Language**: Your body speaks volumes before you even utter a word. Stand tall, with your shoulders back and your head held high. Maintain eye contact with your audience, allowing them to feel seen and engaged. Use purposeful gestures to emphasize your points and convey your passion.

- **Vocal Delivery**: Speak with clarity, enunciating your words and varying your tone and pace to keep your audience engaged. Project your voice to reach every corner of the room, ensuring that your message is heard by all. Embrace pauses for emphasis and to allow your words to sink in.

- **Authenticity**: Be true to yourself and your unique style of speaking. Embrace your strengths and quirks, allowing your genuine personality to shine through. Authenticity breeds confidence, as it shows that you are comfortable in your own skin and have something valuable to offer.

- **Preparation and Practice**: The more you prepare and practice your speech, the more confident you will feel. Rehearse your content, anticipate potential questions or challenges, and be ready with well-thought-out responses. The familiarity with your material will boost your confidence and allow you to adapt seamlessly to any situation.

Remember, confidence is not a destination but a continuous journey. It is something that can be cultivated and nurtured over time. Embrace each speaking opportunity as a chance to grow and learn, and let your confidence evolve with every experience.

Clarity of Thoughts and Ideas

Clarity is not about having all the answers or being a master of every topic. It is the art of distilling complex ideas into simple, understandable concepts that resonate with your audience. It is the ability to articulate your thoughts with precision and purpose, leaving no room for ambiguity or confusion.

As a speaker, clarity is created through a deep understanding of your message. Take the time to clarify your own thoughts and ensure that you have a clear grasp of the key points you want to convey. Ask yourself: What is the core message here that I want to communicate? What are the key takeaways I want my audience to remember? In answering these questions, you lay the foundation for a clear and impactful presentation.

To exhibit clarity of thought as a speaker, consider the following:

- **Structure and Organization**: Craft a well-structured speech that flows logically from one point to another. Begin with a strong introduction that captures your audience's attention and clearly states your main message. Use signposts and transitions to guide your audience through your speech, ensuring that each point is presented in a coherent and organized manner.

- **Language and Vocabulary**: Choose your words carefully, using language that is accessible and relatable to your audience. Avoid jargon or technical terms that may alienate or confuse listeners. Instead, opt for simple, concise, and powerful language that conveys your ideas effectively.

- **Visual Aids**: Utilize visual aids, such as slides or props, to enhance the clarity of your message. Visual representations can help reinforce key points, provide visual cues, and make complex concepts more digestible for your audience. However, be mindful not to overload your presentation with excessive visuals that may distract from your message.

- **Storytelling**: Weave storytelling into your speech to illustrate your ideas and make them more relatable. Stories have the unique power to engage and captivate audiences, allowing them to connect emotionally with your message. Craft compelling narratives that support your main points and help drive home your message with clarity.

By honing your ability to communicate with clarity, you enable your audience to fully grasp and appreciate your message. Remember, clarity of thought is not a one-time achievement but an ongoing pursuit. Continuously refine and simplify your ideas, seeking clarity in every aspect of your communication.

Understanding the Audience

This anecdote is unrelated to public speaking, but I feel compelled to tell it because it will help me illustrate my main point. So, there was a time when I was an active and loyal member of Hinge. To make a long story short, we started talking, and we eventually got to the point and place where we asked each other on the first date. So there I was, eagerly anticipating my first date with this person I met online. We exchanged messages, shared interests, and built a connection that seemed promising. As the day approached, I couldn't help but feel a mix of excitement and nervousness.

When the time came to decide on a venue for our first date, I had a particular place in mind. It was a restaurant known for its exquisite cuisine and elegant ambiance. In my mind, it was the perfect setting for a memorable evening. However, I made a critical mistake—I never communicated the nature of the place to my date.

As we arrived at the restaurant, I noticed a flicker of surprise in their eyes. It was clear that they had not expected such a fancy establishment. At that moment, I realized the importance of understanding your audience and setting appropriate expectations.

You see, just like in public speaking, understanding your audience is crucial. It's about recognizing their preferences, their background, and their expectations. It's about tailoring your message and delivery to resonate with them deeply.

In my case, had I taken the time to understand my date's preferences and communicated the nature of the restaurant, we could have avoided the slight discomfort that arose from the mismatched expectations. It was a valuable lesson that transcended the realm of dating and taught me a fundamental principle of effective communication.

Understanding your audience matters because it is what will help you tailor and make your speech's message In a way that makes it sound like you are speaking to them and not at them. Secondly, it helps you determine what language and tone would be appropriate to use. Different audiences have different levels of familiarity with the topic at hand that you'll be presenting, and using technical jargon or complex terminology may confuse or alienate some listeners. Adapting your language to suit your audience's understanding ensures that you are effectively communicating your ideas and allowing everyone to follow along easily.

You'll also easily be able to identify their interests and concerns. Knowing their background, demographics, and motivations will help you tailor your speech to address their specific needs and capture their attention. This is how a connection is woven between you as the speaker and the audience, making your message more relatable and engaging. When listeners feel that you understand their perspective and are speaking directly to them, they are more likely to remain attentive and receptive to your ideas.

As a speaker, you also have to be able to anticipate any potential objections or questions that may arise during your presentation. If you familiarize yourself with your audience's beliefs, values, and possible doubts, you can proactively address the concerns, providing persuasive arguments or evidence to support your position. You'll establish yourself as credible because they will see that you have taken the time to consider their perspective and are prepared to respond to their reservations.

Some audiences may prefer a more formal and structured approach, while others may respond better to a more informal and interactive style. Do your research and understand what their preferences and expectations are. You can adjust your delivery, like incorporating humor, storytelling, or visual aids, to create a more engaging and memorable experience.

Tips for Understanding Your Audience

- Research your audience: Gather information about their demographics, interests, and knowledge levels to tailor your content accordingly.

- Engage in pre-event conversations: Interact with attendees before your speech to get a sense of their expectations, concerns, and interests.

- Use surveys or questionnaires: Distribute surveys or questionnaires to gather feedback and insights from the audience.

- Observe nonverbal cues: Pay attention to the audience's body language, facial expressions, and reactions during your speech to gauge their level of engagement and understanding.

- Adapt your delivery: Adjust your pace, tone, and language to resonate with the audience and ensure clarity.

- Encourage interaction: Incorporate opportunities for audience participation, such as Q&A sessions or group activities, to foster engagement and gain insights.

Authentic Ways of Speech Delivery

Authenticity is something that cannot be faked. It is the essence of genuine human connection—the bridge that links what we say, how we say it, and what we truly believe. When we speak with conviction, we tap into a wellspring of truth within ourselves, allowing our words to flow with sincerity and conviction.

In a world filled with polished presentations and rehearsed performances, authenticity stands out like a beacon of light. It is the antidote to the superficial and the disingenuous, offering a refreshing and genuine experience for both the speaker and the audience. When we embrace authenticity, we invite others to do the same, creating an atmosphere of trust and openness.

Authenticity is not about perfection or flawless delivery. It is about being true to ourselves, embracing our imperfections, and sharing our unique perspectives and experiences. It is about having the courage to be vulnerable, to let our guard down, and to connect with others on a deeply human level.

When we speak authentically, our words become imbued with a sense of realness and relatability. Our audience can sense the sincerity in our voice, the passion in our words, and the conviction in our beliefs. Authenticity allows us to transcend the boundaries of mere information sharing and engage in meaningful conversations that inspire, motivate, and resonate.

It is not a one-size-fits-all approach. It is an individual journey of self-discovery and self-expression. Every speaker brings their own unique blend of experiences, values, and perspectives to the table. Embracing authenticity means honoring our own voice and allowing it to shine through in our speech, free from the constraints of societal expectations or the desire to please others.

What Would Authenticity Look Like in Different Scenarios?

In personal storytelling, imagine yourself giving a speech about overcoming adversity. An authentic delivery might involve sharing a personal story of a challenging experience you faced, the emotions you felt, and the lessons you learned. By speaking from the heart and connecting your own journey to a broader message of resilience, you create an engaging and relatable experience for your audience.

In an inspirational keynote speech, authenticity can look like sharing a genuine passion for the topic at hand that you're talking about. Let your enthusiasm and belief in the subject shine through as you speak. Use personal anecdotes, impactful quotes, and vivid examples to connect with your audience on an emotional level, inspiring them to take action or embrace a new perspective.

In a panel discussion, authenticity involves active listening, genuine engagement with fellow panelists, and thoughtful responses. Instead of rehearsing answers, speak spontaneously and authentically, sharing your unique insights and perspectives. Show respect for differing opinions and engage in open, honest dialogue, fostering a dynamic and authentic conversation that captivates the audience.

Tips on Speaking More Authentically

- **Know Yourself**: Authenticity begins with self-awareness. Take the time to understand your values, beliefs, and experiences that shape your perspective. This self-knowledge will serve as a foundation for delivering a speech that aligns with your true self.

- **Be Present**: Authenticity thrives in the present moment. Practice mindfulness techniques to stay grounded and fully engaged with your audience. By being present, you can respond authentically to the energy in the room and adapt your speech accordingly.

- **Embrace Vulnerability**: Authenticity requires the courage to be vulnerable. Share personal stories, challenges, and lessons learned. When you open up and show your authentic self, you create a genuine connection with your audience, fostering trust and reliability.

- **Speak From the Heart**: Let your passion and emotions guide your words. Authenticity is not just about the content of your speech but also the way you deliver it. Allow your genuine enthusiasm, conviction, and empathy to shine through, making your message more impactful and memorable.

- **Be Genuine and Natural**: Authenticity thrives when you are true to yourself and avoid putting on a facade. Embrace your natural speaking style, quirks, and mannerisms. Trying to imitate others or forcing a persona will only hinder your authenticity. Let your true self shine through, as it will resonate more deeply with your audience.

- **Share Personal Insights and Lessons**: Authenticity is enhanced when you share personal insights and lessons learned from your own experiences. By weaving in anecdotes and real-life examples, you provide a relatable and authentic perspective. This vulnerability and willingness to share your journey will captivate your audience and make your speech more impactful.

Enthusiasm to Connect With the Audience

In the early years of my career, I remember this colleague that I had. She had this way about her, something infectious; she could get excited about the smallest, most insignificant of things. And the best part about that was her uncanny ability to get you to do the same.

One particular day, our team was tasked with a mundane project that seemed to lack any semblance of excitement. The rest of us were going through the motions, feeling uninspired and unmotivated. But not her. She approached the project with a fiery zest that was both admirable and puzzling. As she shared her ideas and the vision for the project, her eyes sparkled with excitement, and her gestures were animated with passion. She spoke with such conviction and belief that it was impossible not to be drawn into her world of enthusiasm. Suddenly, the project that seemed dull and uninteresting transformed into a canvas of possibilities.

Her enthusiasm was contagious. It spread like wildfire among the team, igniting a newfound energy and creativity within each of us. We began brainstorming ideas, collaborating with fervor, and pushing the boundaries of what we thought was possible. The once-lackluster project became an opportunity for innovation and growth. What truly struck me the most was how her enthusiasm didn't just affect our work but also our overall morale and camaraderie. It created a positive and uplifting atmosphere where everyone felt valued and motivated. We became a team that thrived on enthusiasm, supporting, and inspiring one another to reach new heights.

Looking back, I realized that her enthusiasm wasn't just about being excited for the sake of it. It was a mindset, a way of approaching life and working with passion and purpose. It taught me that enthusiasm is not just a fleeting emotion but a powerful tool that can transform the ordinary into the extraordinary. I made a conscious effort from that day forward to embrace enthusiasm in everything I did. Whether it was speaking in front of a crowd, pitching an idea, or simply engaging in a conversation, I channeled the energy and zest that my colleague had shown me. And I witnessed firsthand the impact it had on my own confidence, engagement, and ability to connect with others.

Enthusiasm became my secret weapon as a speaker. It allowed me to captivate audiences, inspire action, and leave a lasting impression. It became the driving force behind my success, reminding me that when you speak with genuine enthusiasm, you have the power to move hearts and minds.

So, as I reflect on that colleague from years ago, I can't help but feel overwhelmed with gratitude for the invaluable lesson she taught me. Her candor is what turned me into a speaker who appreciates the true power of passion and excitement.

Here's what you can do to amplify and level up your enthusiasm:

- **Use Your Voice**. Speaking is not just a matter of opening up your mouth. It's about variation and using it as an instrument. You can use different elements of your voice, like tone, pitch, volume, and pace. For example, if there is something that you want to emphasize, you can raise your voice up a notch, or if you want to create that element of suspense, you can lower it down a little. Experiment and play around with the different ways in which you can let your enthusiasm shine through.

- **Use Your Body**. When we speak, we are not merely called to share a message but rather to channel our energy and emotion in our bodies so that those words that we are sharing can be a blessing to our audience. For example, use open gestures to show confidence and smile as a way to convey warmth and positivity. Make eye contact to show interest, and move around to show dynamism. There is so much that your body can do. Leverage that and make the most of it.

- Tap into that vast well of emotion. Your emotions are the very essence of your enthusiasm. You need to feel what you want to convey. Use them to show excitement, gratitude, curiosity, and admiration.

- **Repetition Is Key**. You can use it to reinforce your message or to create a memorable climax. For example, you can repeat a word, a phrase, or a sentence throughout your speech, or you can use parallelism or epiphora, a poetic effect.

Have Good Presentation Skills

Imagine stepping onto a stage with all eyes on you, ready to deliver a presentation that leaves your audience in awe. To achieve that, presentation skills are your secret weapon. Let's explore why they matter and how they can transform you into a world-class public speaker.

Picture this: you confidently stride across the stage, your body language exuding charisma. You maintain eye contact, connecting with each person in the audience. Your gestures are purposeful, emphasizing your points and making them come alive. Presentation skills empower you to command attention and create a powerful presence.

But it's not just about how you move; it's about how you speak. Your vocal tone dances with passion, capturing the audience's interest from the very first word. You vary your pitch and pace, keeping them on their toes and hanging onto your every syllable. With presentation skills, your voice becomes a mesmerizing instrument that amplifies your message.

Now let's talk about structure. Your presentation flows seamlessly, like a well-choreographed dance. You organize your ideas in a logical sequence, effortlessly guiding your audience through your story. Your words are clear and concise, avoiding confusing jargon. You want your audience to be captivated, not lost in a sea of complex terms.

Visual aids are your allies in this journey. You wield them with finesse, using striking slides or props that enhance your message. Each visual is carefully chosen, supporting, and reinforcing your words. You strike the perfect balance, ensuring that your visuals don't overpower your presence but rather complement and amplify your impact.

Ah, the audience. They are the heart and soul of your presentation. With presentation skills, you become a master of adaptation. You understand their needs, their interests, and their cultural background. You tailor your content to resonate with them, making it relatable and engaging. You encourage their participation, igniting lively discussions and fostering a sense of connection.

But remember, even the greatest performers rehearse. Presentation skills demand practice. You fine-tune your delivery, polishing every aspect of your performance. You seek feedback, eagerly embracing opportunities for growth. With each rehearsal, you become more comfortable, allowing your authentic self to shine through. In the end, these skills are the key to unlocking your potential as a captivating public speaker. They empower you to leave a lasting impact, to inspire and inform, and to connect with your audience on a profound level.

Tips on Using Visual Aids

- **Simplicity Is Key**. Avoid cluttering your slides with excessive text or complex visuals. Use concise bullet points, relevant images, or graphs to convey your message clearly.

- **Don't Go Overboard With Visuals**. Visual aids should support your presentation, not overshadow it. Use visuals strategically to emphasize key points or illustrate complex concepts.

- **Ensure Readability**. Choose fonts and colors that are easy to read from a distance. Stick to a consistent font style and size throughout your slides. Use contrasting colors for text and background to enhance visibility.

- **Limit Text**: Avoid overwhelming your audience with lengthy paragraphs. Use brief, impactful statements or keywords that capture the essence of your message. Let your spoken words complement the visuals.

- **Incorporate Visuals Beyond Slides**: Consider using props, physical objects, or multimedia elements to engage your audience. These can add a dynamic and interactive dimension to your presentation.

- **Practice With Your Visuals**. Familiarize yourself with the flow of your visual aids during rehearsals. Ensure smooth transitions and timing. Be prepared to navigate through your visuals effortlessly.

- **Be Prepared for Technical Issues**. Have a backup plan in case of technical difficulties. Save your presentation on multiple devices or in the cloud. Consider having printed handouts as a contingency.

- **Customize for Your Audience**. Tailor your visuals to suit the preferences and needs of your audience. Consider their level of knowledge, cultural background, and visual preferences when designing your aids.

- **Seek Feedback**. After your presentation, ask for feedback on the effectiveness of your visual aids. Learn from the experience and make adjustments for future presentations.

Be Prepared for the Unexpected

Anything can happen when you're up on that stage; trust me, I know because I've been there. The unexpected can strike at any moment, throwing you off balance and leaving you scrambling for a solution. That's why you need to be prepared for the unforeseen when delivering a presentation. Let's discuss this and explore some strategies to handle these situations with grace and confidence.

It starts with you acknowledging that the unexpected can occur, which is the first step towards preparedness. Technical glitches, power outages, or even disruptive audience members can disrupt your flow. By accepting that these situations can happen, you can mentally prepare yourself to stay calm and composed, ready to handle whatever comes your way.

One effective strategy is to have a backup plan. Consider having a printed copy of your presentation or notes as a safety net in case of technological failures. This way, you can seamlessly transition to your backup plan without missing a beat. Additionally, familiarize yourself with the venue's equipment and have a contingency plan in case something goes awry.

Another crucial aspect of preparation is anticipating potential questions or challenges from the audience. Take the time to research your topic thoroughly and anticipate possible points of contention. By doing so, you can prepare well-thought-out responses that demonstrate your expertise and maintain control of the situation.

Moreover, practicing improvisation is a valuable skill for handling unexpected moments. Rehearse scenarios where you have to think on your feet and respond spontaneously. This helps build your confidence and adaptability, enabling you to navigate unforeseen circumstances smoothly.

In moments of unexpected disruption, it's essential to maintain composure and engage with the audience. If technical issues arise, use humor or storytelling to keep the audience engaged while the problem is resolved. If an audience member interrupts or asks a challenging question, actively listen, remain respectful, and respond thoughtfully. Remember, the way you handle unexpected situations can leave a lasting impression on your audience.

Additionally, don't be afraid to seek support from event organizers or technical staff. They are there to assist you and can help resolve any issues that arise. Establishing a good rapport with them before your presentation can make it easier to communicate and address any unexpected challenges.

Lastly, reflect on your experiences and learn from them. After each presentation, evaluate what went well and what could have been handled differently. This self-reflection allows you to continuously improve and refine your skills for future presentations.

Maintain Your Sense of Calm

The one thing that we don't often hear enough about is the fact that sometimes when you're up there on that stage doing your thing, you might be met with less than satisfactory responses. The rude audience member who seemingly wants to have a say in everything that you are saying can be quite unsettling. I remember one particular incident when I was delivering a speech on climate change. As I passionately presented my points, a man in the front row began to interrupt, challenging every statement that came from my mouth. His confrontational tone and dismissive remarks could have easily thrown me off balance, but I knew that maintaining my sense of calm was either going to make or break me.

- **Dress for the Occasion**: Consider the context and audience of your speech. Dress slightly more formally than the expected attire to show respect and professionalism.

- **Find Your Power Outfit**: find the outfit that makes you feel like a superstar—the outfit that makes you feel confident and comfortable. When you feel good about what you're wearing, it positively impacts your delivery and stage presence.

- **Pay Attention to Fit**: Make sure your clothes fit well and flatter your body shape. Ill-fitting attire can be distracting and hinder your ability to connect with the audience.

- **Colors and Patterns**: Opt for colors that convey the right message for your speech. Bold colors can exude energy, while neutral tones can project a sense of calmness. Avoid distracting patterns that may divert attention from your message.

- **Mind the Accessories**: Choose accessories that complement your outfit without overpowering it. Simple and tasteful accessories can add a touch of personal style without being distracting.

- **Dress for Comfort**: While looking professional is important, don't sacrifice comfort. Make sure your clothing allows you to move freely and feel at ease on stage. Confidence comes from feeling comfortable in your own skin.

Above all, remember that your clothes is there. To help enhance the message, it's there to help you connect, so choose wisely. Take pride in your appearance, and just watch as you flourish up there on that stage.

Learn How to Modulate Your Voice

If you want to be an engaging speaker, then you're going to have to teach yourself how to speak in a voice that does not seem too rehearsed. But you also still want that speed and inflection that will make your delivery all the more impactful. If you want to work on having the perfect cadence, record yourself and listen to it later. That will give you a better indication of where you sound inauthentic. There are also various techniques that you can try, and these include:

- **Varying Pitch**: Experiment with raising or lowering your pitch to emphasize certain words or ideas. Higher pitches can convey excitement or enthusiasm, while lower pitches can add seriousness or depth.

- **Adjusting Volume**: Use changes in volume to create emphasis and draw attention. Speaking softly can create a sense of intimacy while speaking loudly can command attention and convey passion.

- **Controlling Pace**: Altering the speed at which you speak can help convey different emotions or emphasize important points. Speaking slowly can add weight and significance, while speaking quickly can create a sense of energy or urgency.

- **Utilizing Pauses**: Pauses are powerful tools for emphasizing and allowing your audience to absorb information. Strategic pauses before or after key points can build anticipation and make your message more impactful.

- **Expressing Emotions**: Infuse your voice with appropriate emotions to connect with your audience. Whether it's enthusiasm, empathy, or conviction, letting your emotions come through in your voice can make your delivery more engaging and relatable.

To improve pitch variation, you can also try the following exercises:

- **Humming Scale**: Hum is a simple scale, starting from a comfortable pitch and gradually moving up and down. Focus on smoothly transitioning between the different notes, exploring the full range of your voice.

- **Pitch Slides**: Start with a low pitch and gradually slide your voice up to a high pitch, then slide back down. Repeat this exercise, experimenting with different speeds and intervals.

- **Reading Aloud**: Choose a passage or a poem and read it aloud, paying attention to the pitch variations that naturally occur. Try to emphasize certain words or phrases by adjusting your pitch accordingly.

- **Tongue Twisters**: Practice tongue twisters that involve pitch changes. For example, try saying "Unique New York" with a rising pitch on each word. This exercise helps you become more aware of pitch variations and improves your control.

- **Singing**: Singing exercises, such as vocal warm-ups and scales, can greatly enhance your pitch variation skills. Singing helps you explore different pitches and develop a more flexible vocal range.

Open to Questions by the Public

Okay, so I'm not going to lie. The part that I like the least about this whole public speaking thing is the part where the audience gets to ask you questions. What if somebody asks something that throws me completely off guard, and I embarrass myself right then and there? That was a constant worry of mine when I started speaking. However, I soon learned that any great speaker knows that the talk itself is not really about them but about the audience. It's about connecting with them, engaging them, and providing value. And one powerful way to involve the audience is by asking them questions."

By asking questions, you not only encourage active participation but also create a sense of involvement and connection. It allows the audience to feel heard and valued, and it shows that you genuinely care about their thoughts and opinions. Additionally, asking questions can help you gauge the audience's understanding, tailor your message to their needs, and even uncover valuable insights or perspectives that you may not have considered.

So, instead of fearing questions, embrace them as an opportunity to further engage your audience. Prepare yourself by anticipating potential questions and practicing thoughtful responses. Remember, the goal is not to have all the answers but to foster a meaningful dialogue that enriches the overall experience for both you and your audience.

Tips for Preparing for Unexpected Questions

You're not psychic, so you're never fully going to know what it is that the audience is going to ask you, but using a few tricks and tips, you can prepare yourself for whatever they may throw your way.

Put yourself in their shoes and think about what they might ask. Consider the topic, context, and any controversial or unclear points that may arise.

Research and gather information: Ensure you have a solid understanding of your topic and gather relevant information that may support your responses. This will help you provide well-informed answers.

Practice thinking on your feet by engaging in impromptu speaking exercises. This can help you develop the ability to respond quickly and confidently to unexpected questions.

Identify the key messages or takeaways you want to convey during your speech. Having these points in mind will help you stay focused and provide concise answers even when faced with unexpected questions.

Remember to take a deep breath and maintain a calm demeanor when faced with an unexpected question. Take a moment to gather your thoughts before responding. It's okay to ask for clarification or to take a brief pause if needed.

Redirect if necessary: If you receive a question that is outside the scope of your presentation or not relevant to the topic, politely redirect the conversation back to the main points you want to address. You can say something like, "That's an interesting question, but let's focus on the main topic for now. We can discuss that further later."

Other examples of how you can redirect a question:

Example 1

Audience Member: "What are your thoughts on the recent political developments?"

Speaker: "Thank you for your question. While political developments are certainly important, today's presentation is focused on discussing effective communication strategies in the workplace. However, I'd be happy to connect with you after the session to discuss politics further if you'd like."

In this scenario, you appreciate the question's relevance but gently redirect the conversation back to the main topic of the presentation. By offering to address the question outside the current context, you show respect for the audience member's inquiry while staying on track with the intended focus of the presentation.

Example 2

Audience Member: "Can you provide specific statistics to support your claims?"

Speaker: "Thank you for your question. While I don't have the specific statistics on hand at the moment, I can assure you that our claims are backed by extensive research and data. I'd be happy to share the sources and provide more detailed information after the presentation."

In this example, you acknowledge the request for specific statistics but acknowledge that they don't have them readily available. You do, however, still assure the audience member that their claims are supported by research and offer to share the sources and provide more information later. This response shows transparency, confidence, and a willingness to provide additional evidence outside the scope of the presentation.

It takes work to be a great speaker. Sure, you can be talented, but that will only get you so far. To truly excel in the realm of public speaking requires dedication, practice, and continuous improvement.

Talent may provide a natural inclination towards effective communication, but it is through deliberate effort that one hones one's skills and becomes a truly exceptional speaker. It's like any other craft or art form—while some individuals may have a head start, it is the commitment to constant growth and refinement that sets apart the truly remarkable speakers from the rest. So embrace the work that it takes and commit yourself to constant growth and improvement.

Chapter 5:

Benefits of Mastering Public

Speaking Skills

I love a great life hack. I love discovering that I can use something like a grater to juice my lemons and not just to grate my cheese or that I can keep my white sneakers white and dazzling by mixing a little bit of bicarbonate of soda with my washing powder. Public speaking, in its own way, is like one of these incredible life hacks.

I remember the first time I had to give a presentation in front of a large audience. My heart raced, my palms became sweaty, and my mind went blank. I stumbled through my words, barely able to maintain eye contact with anyone in the room. It was a nerve-wracking experience, to say the least.

But then I decided to tackle my fear head-on. I enrolled in a public speaking course, determined to transform myself into a confident and captivating speaker. Little did I know that this decision would be a life hack that would unlock a world of benefits.

As I learned the techniques and practiced my speaking skills, I began to notice a shift within me. With each presentation, my confidence grew, and the fear that once paralyzed me started to dissipate. I discovered that public speaking was not just about delivering information; it was about connecting with the audience, engaging their emotions, and leaving a lasting impact.

This newfound confidence spilled over into other areas of my life. I found myself speaking up more in meetings, sharing my ideas without hesitation, and even taking on leadership roles. The ability to communicate effectively became my secret weapon, a life hack that propelled me forward in both personal and professional endeavors.

In my career, I witnessed the power of public speaking firsthand. Whether it was pitching a new idea to clients, delivering a keynote address at a conference, or leading a team meeting, my ability to articulate my thoughts clearly and persuasively set me apart. I became known as the go-to person for presentations and public speaking engagements, opening doors to exciting opportunities and advancement.

But it wasn't just about personal gain. I realized that public speaking allowed me to make a difference in the lives of others. Whether it was inspiring a room full of students, motivating colleagues to embrace change, or advocating for a cause close to my heart, I saw the impact my words could have on others. Public speaking became a life hack, not just for my own success but for positively influencing those around me.

So, just like that ingenious life hack that turns a grater into a lemon juicer, mastering public speaking is a skill that can change the trajectory of your whole life, and in this whole chapter, we explore how you can make it work harder for you.

Helps in Career Advancement

Nobody wants to find themselves in the same place that they were after five years. We all want growth. We all want progress in some way or another. And let me let you in on a little secret. You can make that progress if you know how to speak up and how to show up for your desires. Public speaking is something that can help you get there.

Imagine a scenario where you have a brilliant idea, a groundbreaking solution, or a unique perspective that could potentially change the game. You have the knowledge, the skills, and the passion, but without the ability to effectively communicate and share your ideas, they remain locked within you, unable to make an impact. This is where public speaking comes in as a powerful tool for personal and professional growth.

When you master the art of public speaking, you unlock a world of possibilities. It goes beyond simply conveying information or delivering a speech. Public speaking is about connecting, capturing attention, and leaving a lasting impression. It's also about confidently expressing your thoughts, ideas, and expertise in a way that resonates with others, and one of the key benefits of this is its impact on career advancement. In today's competitive world, effective communication skills are highly sought after by employers. The ability to articulate ideas clearly, engage an audience, and deliver compelling presentations can set you apart from your peers. It opens doors to new opportunities, promotions, and leadership roles. It helps you build confidence, showcase your expertise, and establish yourself as a credible and influential professional.

Let's not forget how it enhances your leadership abilities. It equips you with the skills to inspire and motivate others, to lead with conviction, and to influence positive change. Whether you're leading a team, spearheading a project, or advocating for a cause, the ability to communicate your vision and rally others behind it is crucial; it's how you develop a presence that demands attention.

Tips on Using Your Public Speaking Skills to Network and Influence

If you've mastered the art or the craft, why not allow it to do the heavy lifting? You don't always have to work the hardest out of everyone, but you can always choose to work smarter than the rest. Here are some tips that you can pocket to help you use your public speaking skills to network and influence:

- **Craft an Elevator Pitch**: Your public speaking skills can help you create a compelling elevator pitch—a concise and persuasive introduction that captures attention and sparks interest. For example, imagine you're attending a networking event. Instead of simply saying, "Hi, I'm John, I work in marketing," you can use your public speaking skills to confidently say, "Hi, I'm John, and I specialize in creating data-driven marketing strategies that drive exponential growth. Let me share with you how I helped a startup increase its customer base by 50% in just three months.

- **Engage in Panel Discussions**: Participating in panel discussions allows you to showcase your expertise and connect with industry professionals. You can contribute valuable insights, engage in meaningful conversations, and leave a lasting impression. For instance, imagine you're on a panel discussing the future of renewable energy. Using your public speaking skills, you can confidently share your research findings and present innovative ideas that captivate the audience and position you as a thought leader in the field.

- **Host Workshops**: Hosting workshops or webinars allows you to share your knowledge and expertise with a targeted audience. Use your public speaking skills to engage participants, facilitate discussions, and provide valuable insights. For instance, if you're hosting a workshop on leadership development, you can use your public speaking skills to deliver engaging activities, encourage participants to share their experiences, and provide practical tips that empower them to become better leaders.

- **Offer to Speak**: at industry conferences, seminars, or community events to expand your network and influence. Leverage your public speaking skills to deliver impactful presentations that resonate with the audience. So, if you're passionate about environmental sustainability, you can volunteer as a speaker at a sustainability conference, sharing your insights on sustainable practices and inspiring others to take action.

- **Leverage Your Social Media Platforms**: In today's digital age, social media platforms provide a powerful avenue to network and influence. Use your public speaking skills to create engaging video content, deliver informative webinars, or participate in live Q&A sessions. For instance, you can host a live webinar on LinkedIn, sharing your expertise on a specific topic and engaging with professionals from around the world.

Tips on Using Your Public Speaking Skills to Build Your Personal Brand

Your personal brand as a speaker, as an entrepreneur, or as anyone in business really matters. So you mustn't be lazy to build it. You have to take a radical and unconventional approach. Here are a few tips to help you:

- **Define Your Unique Voice**: Your public speaking skills can help you define and amplify your unique voice, setting you apart from others in your industry. For example, if you're a fitness enthusiast, you can build motivational speeches that inspire others to live a healthy lifestyle, showcasing your expertise and passion.

- **Share With Value**: Use your skills to create and share valuable content that aligns with your personal brand. Whether it's through podcasts, YouTube videos, or live presentations, leverage your skills to deliver insightful and informative content. Let's say you work in marketing. You can create video tutorials on effective marketing strategies, positioning yourself as a go-to resource in the industry.

- **Two Words**: thought leadership. Public speaking allows you to position yourself as a thought leader in your field. Leverage your skills to speak at industry conferences, contribute to panel discussions, or publish articles in relevant publications. By opening yourself up and sharing your expertise and insights, you can establish yourself as a trusted authority. For example, if you're a technology expert, you can deliver keynote speeches at tech conferences, sharing your vision for the future of the industry.

- **Network With Intention and Purpose**: Attend industry events, join professional organizations, and actively engage with others. Leverage your skills to confidently introduce yourself, share your personal brand story, and make meaningful connections. For instance, when attending a networking event, use your public speaking skills to engage in conversations that highlight your expertise and leave a lasting impression.

Social media platforms have revolutionized the way in which we do business today because they provide a powerful avenue for us to build our personal brand. Use your skills to create engaging video content, host live Q&A sessions, or participate in Twitter chats. For example, if you're a fashion influencer, you can use your public speaking skills to create captivating videos showcasing your unique style, sharing fashion tips, and engaging with your audience.

Actively seek speaking opportunities that align with your personal brand. This could include speaking at local events, webinars, or even hosting your own workshops. Leverage your public speaking skills to deliver impactful presentations that resonate with your target audience. For instance, if you're a career coach, you can offer workshops on personal branding and professional development, showcasing your expertise and building your personal brand as a trusted career advisor.

It Promotes Awareness

Public speaking is not just about delivering speeches or presentations; it has the power to promote awareness and ignite change. When you step onto that stage or stand in front of an audience, you have the opportunity to shed light on important issues, spark conversations, and inspire action.

One way public speaking promotes awareness is by bringing attention to social causes. Whether it's advocating for environmental sustainability, raising awareness about mental health, or fighting for social justice, public speaking allows individuals to use their voices to amplify important messages. By sharing personal stories, statistics, and compelling arguments, speakers can captivate audiences and inspire them to take action.

Imagine a passionate environmentalist delivering a TED talk on the urgency of climate change. Through their public speaking skills, they can effectively communicate the consequences of inaction, share innovative solutions, and motivate others to make sustainable choices. By raising awareness about the environment, they encourage individuals to become more conscious of their impact and take steps towards a greener future.

Public speaking also promotes awareness by providing a platform for marginalized voices. It allows individuals from underrepresented communities to share their experiences, challenges, and perspectives with a wider audience. By giving a voice to those who have been silenced or overlooked, public speaking can challenge societal norms, break down stereotypes, and foster empathy and understanding.

For example, a speaker who identifies as LGBTQ+ can use their public speaking skills to share their personal journey, educate others about the challenges faced by the community, and advocate for acceptance and equality. By sharing their story, they promote awareness about LGBTQ+ issues, encourage empathy, and contribute to a more inclusive society. It also raises awareness about lesser-known topics or niche areas of interest. It allows experts in various fields to share their knowledge and insights, shedding light on subjects that may not receive mainstream attention. By delivering engaging presentations, workshops, or webinars, they can educate and inspire audiences, expanding their understanding of the world.

Consider a scientist who specializes in marine biology. Through public speaking, they can educate the public about the importance of ocean conservation, the impact of pollution on marine life, and the need for sustainable practices.

Empowers Leadership Qualities

Warren Bennis said it best when he defined leadership as the capacity to translate vision into reality. And in some way or another, public speaking plays a vital role in making that translation possible. It is through the power of effective communication that leaders can inspire, influence, and bring their visions to life.

Imagine a leader with a grand vision—a transformative idea that has the potential to change the world. However, without the ability to effectively communicate that vision, it remains confined within their own minds, unable to inspire others or drive meaningful change. This is where public speaking steps in as a crucial tool for leaders.

Public speaking empowers us to articulate our vision with clarity, passion, and conviction. It allows us to connect with each other and share our passion and commitment. Through the art of public speaking, we can paint a vivid picture of the future we envision, igniting a sense of purpose and inspiring others to join them on the journey.

One of the keyways public speaking promotes awareness is by enabling leaders to effectively communicate complex ideas and concepts. Whether it's addressing a large audience, delivering a TED talk, or engaging in a panel discussion, leaders can use their public speaking skills to break down complex topics into digestible and relatable messages. By simplifying and conveying information in a compelling manner, leaders can raise awareness and foster understanding among their audience. We must not forget as well that public speaking is something that helps us advocate for causes and issues that matter to us. It is how we can shine a light on social, environmental, or economic challenges, bringing attention to important matters and mobilizing others to take action.

And lastly, by providing us with a platform to share their expertise and insight, we can educate their audience, share valuable knowledge, and offer fresh perspectives. This not only promotes awareness but also positions leaders as credible authorities in their respective fields, enhancing their influence and impact.

Leadership is something that requires consciousness and awareness— you can be a good, great leader if you roll up your sleeves and commit to doing the character work that it requires. Here are some things that you can focus on to enhance your confidence as a leader.

- Understand your areas of lack and your areas of abundance: Identify your unique skills and qualities as a leader.

Understanding your strengths will boost your confidence and allow you to leverage them accordingly.

- Be a realistic goal-setter: Set clear, attainable goals for yourself as a leader. You know what limitations you have and what your capabilities are, so use those to set clear, intentional goals.

- Value feedback: Regularly seek feedback from your team, peers, and superiors. This will give valuable insights into areas where you excel and areas where you can improve, ultimately boosting your confidence.

- Invest in your personal and professional development by attending workshops, courses, or conferences related to leadership. Expanding your knowledge and skills will increase your confidence because you've got more to share, to teach, and to give.

- You are just as good as your community of people, and great leaders know that success is a journey they can't walk on their own. Build a strong support network of mentors, coaches, or peers who can provide guidance and encouragement. Having a support system will help you navigate challenges and boost your confidence.

- Take time to reflect on your experiences and learn from them. Celebrate your successes and identify areas for improvement. This self-awareness will enhance your confidence as a leader.

- Step outside your comfort zone and take calculated risks. Pushing yourself to try new things and embrace challenges will build your confidence in your ability to handle different situations.

- Don't be a hypocrite. Demonstrate the behaviors and qualities you expect from those you are leading.

- Acknowledge and celebrate in times of victory, no matter how big or small. This will reinforce your belief in your capabilities and give you the enthusiasm to keep working on yourself.

- You cannot give if you're running on empty. Take care of your physical and mental well-being. Prioritize self-care activities such as exercise, healthy eating, relaxation techniques, and maintaining a healthy work-life balance. When you feel your best, your confidence as a leader will naturally increase.

Makes One an Active Listener

Active listening is a skill that, quite frankly, most of us still need to work on. I remember sitting across this couple in a cozy coffee shop a while back. As I sipped my latte, I couldn't help but notice their animated conversation. The man—let's call him Mark—was passionately sharing his latest hiking adventure, complete with vivid descriptions of breathtaking landscapes and heart-pounding encounters with wildlife. Meanwhile, his partner, Sarah, seemed lost in her own world, absentmindedly nodding, and occasionally interjecting with a distracted "uh-huh."

Curiosity piqued, and I couldn't resist eavesdropping on their conversation. Mark's enthusiasm was infectious, and I found myself getting caught up in his tales of adventure. But as I glanced at Sarah, I couldn't help but notice her eyes wandering and her mind seemingly elsewhere. It was as if she was physically present but mentally absent.

Suddenly, Mark paused mid-sentence and looked at Sarah expectantly. "So, what do you think?" he asked, a hint of anticipation in his voice. Sarah blinked, momentarily startled, before offering a vague response that had little to do with what Mark had just shared. It was clear that she hadn't been actively listening.

The moment stuck with me, serving as a reminder of the importance of active listening. Mark had poured his heart and soul into recounting his thrilling experiences, hoping for a genuine connection with Sarah. Yet her lack of engagement left him feeling unheard and unappreciated.

This incident made me realize that active listening is not just about hearing the words someone says; it's about being fully present and engaged in the conversation. It's about showing genuine interest, asking thoughtful questions, and providing meaningful responses. Active listening allows us to truly understand and connect with others, fostering stronger relationships and deeper understanding.

Now, public speaking and active listening are two sides of the same coin, each enhancing the other in a beautiful dance of communication. When we step into the spotlight to deliver a speech or presentation, we naturally become more attuned to our audience. We observe their reactions, gauge their engagement, and adjust our delivery accordingly. This heightened awareness among our listeners fosters a deeper understanding of the importance of active listening.

When we're up there on the stage, we experience firsthand the impact of being heard and understood. We witness the power of genuine engagement and connection with our audience. We see their faces light up when we share a relatable story or make them laugh with a well-timed joke. We feel the energy in the room when our words resonate and inspire. These moments remind us that communication is a two-way street, and active listening is the key that unlocks its true potential.

We learn the value of being fully present and attentive. We recognize that it's not just about delivering a monologue but about creating a dialogue with our listeners. We understand that active listening is not just about hearing words but about understanding the emotions, intentions, and underlying messages behind them. When we become more skilled at public speaking, we naturally become better active listeners. We develop the ability to truly listen, not just with our ears but with our hearts and minds. We learn to ask thoughtful questions, seek clarification, and provide meaningful responses. We become more empathetic by putting ourselves in the shoes of our audience and understanding their perspectives, and this reciprocal relationship is a powerful force. It transforms our communication skills, making us more effective and engaging speakers while also cultivating our ability to connect deeply with others. It creates a positive feedback loop where each skill reinforces and strengthens the other.

Active Listening Tips for Public Speaking

- Maintain eye contact and use nonverbal cues to show engagement: By making eye contact with the audience and using gestures or nods, you convey that you are actively listening and interested in what they have to say.

- Restating or summarizing someone's points shows that you are actively processing the information and helps ensure that you have correctly understood their message.

- Ask clarifying questions to ensure comprehension and active listening. When you ask questions to seek clarification, it demonstrates that you are actively engaged and interested in fully understanding their perspective.

- Avoid interrupting or rushing through responses; allow them to fully express their thoughts: Give them time to express their ideas without interrupting or rushing them. This shows respect for their opinions and encourages open dialogue.

- Empathize with them. Displaying empathy and genuine interest helps create a positive and supportive environment, making the audience more comfortable sharing their thoughts and ideas with you.

Will it be easy to ease yourself into that process of fully becoming comfortable with being in front of people? No, it's not going to be, but when it does get hard, remind yourself of the many wonderful benefits that you'll reap. Think of this talent and raft as a gift that you'll give yourself, who'll continue giving back to you over and over again as you continue to grow, both personally and professionally.

Chapter 6:

Challenges on the Path of Being a

Public Speaker

I used to be one of those people who believed that if you find something that you love doing, something that you're incredibly passionate about, then no day would be a challenge. Every day would be a breeze, and boy, oh boy, was I wrong. That is why I want to shed light on the struggles, because I think that the more we talk about these hard bits, the less alone we'll feel through the less glamorous bits.

Delivering Quality Content

I love the crafting and creation process behind creating a speech, but does that mean it's easy? Hardly because the singular most frequent question that pops up in my mind is this: Is this quality content? Is this the kind of content that I would appreciate listening to?

I want you to picture this: It was a crisp autumn evening, and I found myself seated among a crowd of eager listeners in a grand auditorium. The anticipation in the air was palpable as the renowned public speaker took the stage. Little did I know that the next hour would be an unforgettable journey of inspiration and enlightenment.

As the speaker began, I was immediately struck by their confident presence and commanding voice. But it wasn't just their delivery that held my attention; it was the substance of their words that truly captivated me. Each sentence was carefully crafted and packed with valuable insights and thought-provoking ideas. It was like a symphony of words resonating deep within me.

Throughout the speech, the speaker effortlessly weaved personal anecdotes, real-life examples, and relevant statistics into a tapestry of knowledge. They painted vivid pictures with their words, transporting us to different worlds and making complex concepts accessible to all. It was a masterclass in storytelling, as every anecdote served a purpose, illustrating key points and engaging the audience on an emotional level.

But what truly set this speaker apart was their unwavering commitment to delivering quality content. It was evident that they had invested countless hours researching, refining, and curating their material. They had a deep understanding of their audience's needs and tailored their content accordingly. They didn't just scratch the surface; they dug deep into the subject matter, providing valuable insights, and leaving no stone unturned.

As I sat there, engrossed in every word, I couldn't help but reflect on my own journey as a speaker. I realized that crafting quality content is not a task for the faint of heart. It requires dedication, passion, and a relentless pursuit of excellence. The singular most frequent question that pops up in my mind is this: Is this quality content? Is this the kind of content that I would enjoy listening to?

That unforgettable evening taught me that quality content is the lifeblood of any impactful speech. It is the foundation upon which great speakers are built. It is the key that unlocks the minds and hearts of the audience, leaving a lasting impression.

Tips for Researching and Curating Your Material

When it comes to crafting a powerful and engaging speech, there's no denying that quality content is king (or queen). And, as with any type of content creation, your research process plays a crucial role in setting the stage for success. Whether you're working on something for the next big presentation, a TED talk, or just a casual gathering, taking the time to do thorough research will help you hone in on the most important points and craft a message that truly resonates with your audience. So, where do you begin? I'll let you in on a few secrets:

- **Define Your Objective**: Clearly understand the purpose and message of your speech. This will help you focus your research efforts on finding relevant and valuable information.

- **Use Credible Sources**: Rely on reputable sources such as academic journals, books, trusted websites, and expert interviews. Verify the credibility and accuracy of the information before including it in your speech.

- **Organize Your Research**: Create a system to organize your research materials, whether it's using digital tools like note-taking apps or traditional methods like index cards. This will make it easier to retrieve and reference information during the speechwriting process.

- **Be Selective**: Not all the information you find during research needs to be included in your speech. Choose the most compelling, relevant, and impactful points that align with your objective and resonate with your audience.

- **Provide Variety**: Incorporate a mix of statistics, anecdotes, case studies, and examples to make your content engaging and relatable. This variety keeps your audience interested and helps illustrate your points effectively.

- **Attribute Your Sources**: Give credit to the original authors or sources of the information you include in your speech. This adds credibility to your content and shows respect for intellectual property.

- **Don't Just Accept Everything at Face Value**: Analyze and evaluate the information you gather during research. Consider different perspectives, question assumptions, and ensure that the information aligns with your message and supports your arguments.

- **Stay Up-To-Date**: Depending on the topic, it's essential to stay updated with the latest research and developments. This ensures that your content is current and relevant.

Make Sure That Your Source Is Credible

Look, when you're going to be delivering something that is heavily fact-based, you want to make sure that your source isn't just some lad or girl behind a computer screen who reads a couple of articles and now thinks that they are some expert. Here are some things to consider to ensure they are all credible.

- Check the credentials, expertise, and reputation of the author or organization responsible for the source. Look for their qualifications, affiliations, and experience in the field.

- If the source is from a scholarly journal or academic publication, it's likely to have undergone a rigorous peer-review process. This indicates that experts in the field have evaluated and approved the content.

- Think about the reputation and reliability of the publication or website hosting the source. Established and well-known publishers or reputable institutions tend to maintain higher standards of accuracy and credibility.

- Citations and references: Look for sources that provide citations and references to support the information presented. This allows you to verify the accuracy and credibility of the claims made.

- Objectivity and bias: Assess whether the source presents information objectively or if it has a clear bias or agenda. Balanced and unbiased sources are generally more credible as they strive to provide a fair and accurate representation of the topic.

- Check the publication date of the source to ensure it is up-to-date. Depending on the subject matter, it's important to consider the reliability of the information to ensure its relevance and accuracy.

- Cross-reference the information with other credible sources to see if there is consistency in the facts and findings. Multiple reliable sources supporting similar information increase its credibility.

- Peer consensus and citations: If the source has been cited and referenced by other reputable authors or publications, it indicates that it is considered credible within the academic or professional community.

Final Tips on Delivering Quality Content

Structure your content: Organize your speech in a logical and coherent manner. Use a clear introduction, body, and conclusion to guide your audience through your ideas and ensure they can follow your message easily.

Keep it concise: Respect your audience's time and attention span by delivering content that is concise and to the point. Avoid unnecessary jargon or lengthy explanations that may confuse or bore your listeners.

Provide actionable takeaways: Offer practical and actionable advice or insights that your audience can apply in their own lives. This helps them see the value in your content and encourages them to take action.

Accept constructive criticism. You can do this by approaching people you trust, such as mentors, colleagues, or friends who have experience in public speaking or communication. Their insights can provide valuable perspectives on your content delivery. Alternatively, consider working with a professional speech coach or consultant who specializes in content delivery. They can provide personalized feedback, identify areas for improvement, and offer techniques to enhance your delivery skills. If you will be delivering a speech at an event or workshop, ask the organizers if they provide feedback forms or evaluations. This will allow attendees to provide specific feedback on your content delivery, which can be a reference for future improvements.

Handling Negative Feedbacks

Look, I am not going to lie, and I can be a bit of a sore loser. Before you jump to any conclusion, I first want to mention that I am not one of those petty people who'll throw a tantrum when they don't get the feedback that they want. I just mean that I don't take too kindly to negative feedback. I want people to spare my feelings. To sugarcoat things and lace them in syrup. I vividly recall the time I participated in an orator competition during my school years. As the day of the event approached, my nerves grew increasingly jittery. I had spent countless hours preparing my speech, meticulously crafting each word to perfection. However, deep down, I secretly hoped for nothing but praise and admiration from the judges and audience.

The day of the competition arrived, and I took my place on the stage, my heart pounding in my chest like a big, fat African drum. I delivered my speech with passion and conviction, pouring my soul and spirit into every word. The audience seemed engaged, nodding along and occasionally offering encouraging smiles. I felt a glimmer of hope that my efforts would be rewarded. But when the time came for the judges' feedback, I was met with a mixture of positive and negative comments. One judge commended my delivery and stage presence, while another criticized my lack of supporting evidence. It felt like a big fat punch to the gut, and I could feel my face flush with embarrassment. In that moment, I had a choice to make. I could let the negative feedback consume me, allowing it to shatter my confidence and discourage me from ever speaking in public again. Or, I could use it as an opportunity for growth and improvement.

I took a deep breath and reminded myself that feedback, even the negative kind, is a valuable gift. It provides an outsider's perspective, highlighting areas where I can refine my skills. Instead of dwelling on the criticism, I chose to focus on the constructive aspects of the feedback.

I sought out the judge, who pointed out my lack of supporting evidence and asked for further guidance. I wanted to understand how I could strengthen that aspect of my speech. The judge, appreciating my willingness to learn, offered valuable insights and suggested resources to enhance my research skills.

Embracing the feedback, I committed myself to practice and improvement. I sought out opportunities to speak in front of smaller audiences, honing my ability to present compelling arguments supported by solid evidence. Over time, I grew more comfortable receiving feedback, recognizing it as an essential part of my growth as a public speaker.

Looking back, that experience taught me a valuable lesson about handling negative feedback. It's not about seeking validation or having every word praised but rather about using feedback as a stepping stone to becoming a better speaker.

Take Constructive Criticism Like a Champ

Receiving negative feedback can be challenging because it often feels like a personal attack on our abilities or efforts. We naturally seek validation and want to be praised, so when faced with criticism, it can bruise our ego, making us question our worth. Also, there's something about negative feedback that can trigger feelings of defensiveness and vulnerability because it highlights areas where we may need to improve or change. It takes a certain level of self-awareness and openness to accept and learn from negative feedback.

Overcoming that fear of receiving negative feedback requires a shift in mindset and a proactive approach. Here is what you can do:

Embrace a Growth Mindset

A growth mindset says, "Well, this may not have gone as I wished it would, but tomorrow, I can try again, and I will be better." Negative feedback is just an opportunity for growth and improvement. See it as valuable input to help you develop your skills and reach your full potential. Just because they did not necessarily like what you delivered or presented does not mean that you aren't good or talented.

Separate Feedback From Self-Worth

Feedback plays a big role in how we perceive our self-worth. It gives validation and acceptance, serving as external confirmation of one's value and abilities. It is that declaration: "Yes, you are good. You are talented; you are worthy." That we so want to hear. Positive feedback can boost self-esteem and reinforce a sense of worthiness, while negative feedback, on the other hand, can lead to feelings of inadequacy and a diminished sense of self. Let's not forget about the social comparison it triggers, which impacts our self-worth, because if you don't receive the same feedback as someone else, then there must be something wrong with you, right?

This attachment of self-worth to feedback is often rooted in a desire for external validation and acceptance. From a young age, we are conditioned to seek approval from authority figures, leading to a reliance on feedback as a measure of self-worth. Personal identity is closely tied to the feedback received on specific qualities or skills. Positive feedback on areas that we strongly identify with can reinforce our self-worth, while negative feedback can undermine the confidence we've worked so hard to build. However, it is important to recognize that relying solely on external feedback for self-worth can be problematic because it can create a fragile sense of self and a constant need for validation.

You have to work on reminding yourself that feedback is about your work or performance, not your personal value as a person. Detaching your self-esteem from feedback can make it easier to accept and process.

Seek Feedback Proactively

Actively seek feedback from trusted sources, such as mentors, colleagues, or experts in your field. By seeking feedback regularly, you become more accustomed to receiving it and can learn to appreciate its value.

Focus on the Constructive Aspects

Here's the thing that usually happens when you're receiving feedback: You're brain completely disregards everything else that was said, and it moves to the not-so-savory good parts. And that's what makes us ruminate and what makes us feel so miserable at times. Instead of dwelling on the negative aspects of feedback, concentrate on the constructive elements. Look for specific suggestions or areas for improvement that can help you grow and develop.

Practice Active Listening

When receiving feedback, practice active listening by fully engaging with the feedback provider. Seek clarification, ask questions, and show genuine interest in understanding their perspective. This can help you see feedback as a learning opportunity rather than a personal attack.

Take Time to Process

If negative feedback initially stings, give yourself time to process it. Avoid reacting impulsively or defensively. Take a step back, reflect on the feedback, and consider how it aligns with your goals and aspirations.

Celebrate

Look, sure, the feedback that you got might be less than you wanted or expected it to be, but you showed up and were present on that stage, weren't you? That is something bad. Something that deserves to be applauded and appreciated. Recognize that receiving feedback, even if negative, is a sign of progress. It means you are putting yourself out there, taking risks, and seeking growth. Celebrate your courage and resilience in embracing feedback as part of your journey.

Here are some examples that you can draw some wisdom and inspiration from to help you:

Example 1

A fellow speaker provides feedback on your presentation, suggesting that you could improve your body language and gestures.

Positive response: "Thank you for your feedback! I value your insights. I will focus on refining my body language and gestures to enhance my overall delivery and engage the audience more effectively."

Example 2

An audience member shares feedback about your speech, mentioning that the introduction could be more attention-grabbing.

Positive response: "I appreciate your feedback. Capturing the audience's attention from the start is crucial. I will work on crafting a more compelling introduction to create a stronger impact and set the tone for my speeches."

Example 3

A coach provides feedback on your vocal projection during a practice session, suggesting that you could project your voice with more confidence and clarity.

Positive response: "Thank you for your feedback. I understand the importance of projecting my voice effectively. I will practice vocal exercises and techniques to improve my confidence and ensure clearer communication during my speeches."

Example 4

A mentor offers feedback on your use of visual aids, mentioning that you could enhance their relevance and visual appeal.

Positive response: "I'm grateful for your feedback. Visual aids play a significant role in supporting my message. I will take your suggestions into consideration and work on creating more relevant and visually appealing visuals to enhance my presentations."

Example 5

A peer speaker provides feedback on your pacing, suggesting that you could vary your speed to add more emphasis and maintain audience engagement.

Positive response: "Thank you for sharing your feedback. Pacing is an essential aspect of effective speaking. I will practice incorporating variations in speed to create more impact and keep the audience engaged throughout my speeches."

Distracting Audience

A distractive audience member can be a particularly tricky thing to deal with. I mean, just imagine you're up there on the stage, trying to deliver a captivating speech at a prestigious conference. The room is filled with eager faces, all eyes on you. As you begin to speak, you notice a man in the front row—let's call him Mr. Distraction—who seems to have a knack for diverting attention.

Mr. Distraction, clad in a vibrant Hawaiian shirt, decides to engage in a lively conversation with his neighbor. Their voices rise above your carefully crafted words, creating a dissonant symphony that threatens to drown out your message. You take a deep breath, reminding yourself of the importance of maintaining composure.

Undeterred, you continue with your speech, hoping to regain the audience's attention. But then Mr. Distraction pulls out his phone and starts scrolling through social media, his bright screen illuminating his face like a beacon of distraction. The glow catches the eyes of those around him, drawing their attention away from your carefully crafted words.

Now faced with the dual challenge of competing with both conversation and technology, you must think on your feet. You decide to incorporate audience participation by asking a thought-provoking question that requires their engagement. By doing so, you redirect their focus back to you, creating a momentary respite from Mr. Distraction's antics.

As you continue, you notice that Mr. Distraction's neighbor, growing tired of the disruption, leans over and whispers something to him. Mr. Distraction, seemingly caught off guard, finally realizes the impact of his actions. He sheepishly puts his phone away and leans in attentively, ready to listen.

In that moment, you realize the power of persistence and adaptability. Despite the challenges posed by a distractive audience member, you managed to regain control of the room and deliver your message with conviction. The experience serves as a reminder that even in the face of distractions, you, as a skilled speaker, can still find ways to engage and captivate, even if the circumstances are less than perfect.

Common Disruptions From the Audience

- **Side Conversations**: Politely address the entire audience and ask a thought-provoking question to redirect their attention back to your speech.

- **Mobile Devices**: Encourage the use of a designated "phone-free" zone or politely remind the audience to silence their devices at the beginning of your speech.

- **Noise or Movement**: Maintain a confident and engaging presence on stage, using vocal variety and gestures to capture attention. If necessary, pause and wait for the noise or movement to subside before continuing.

- **Latecomers**: Acknowledge latecomers briefly and then refocus on your speech. Avoid letting their arrival disrupt your flow or concentration.

- **Visual Distractions**: Minimize distractions on stage, such as excessive props or clutter, that may divert attention away from your message. Use visual aids strategically to enhance understanding, not overwhelm.

How Do You Handle These Situations?

- **Stay Composed**: Maintain your composure and avoid showing frustration or irritation. Stay focused on your message and project confidence.

- **Engage the Audience**: Incorporate interactive elements, such as questions, activities, or stories, to keep the audience engaged and minimize distractions.

- **Adapt Your Delivery**: Vary your speaking style, pace, and tone to recapture attention. Use pauses strategically to regain control and refocus the audience's attention.

- **Use Eye Contact**: Establish eye contact with attentive audience members to create a connection and draw attention back to your speech.

- **Seek Support If Needed**: If distractions persist or become disruptive, discreetly communicate with event organizers or staff for assistance in managing the situation.

Remember, maintaining audience engagement and managing distractions is a skill that improves with practice. By being proactive and adaptable, you can effectively handle common distractions and deliver a successful speech.

Tips on Dealing With Distractive Audience Members

- **Stay Focused**: Remind yourself of the importance of your message and stay committed to delivering it despite distractions. Maintain eye contact with attentive audience members to regain your confidence.

- **Address the Distraction Indirectly**: Instead of singling out the distracting individual, address the entire audience with a question or interactive activity that encourages engagement. This can help redirect attention and involve everyone in the discussion.

- **Use Humor Strategically**: Injecting a well-timed, light-hearted remark can help diffuse tension and regain control of the room. However, be cautious not to overuse humor or offend anyone in the process.

- **Maintain a Calm Demeanor**: Project confidence and composure by controlling your body language and voice. Take deep breaths, speak clearly, and maintain a steady pace, showing that you are in control of the situation.

- **Seek Support From Event Organizers**: If the distraction persists and significantly hampers your ability to deliver your speech, discreetly communicate with event organizers or staff. They can assist in managing the situation or addressing the distracting individual.

- **Practice Resilience**: Understand that distractions are a part of public speaking and that even experienced speakers encounter them. Develop resilience by practicing your speech in various scenarios, including ones with potential distractions, to build your ability to adapt and stay focused.

Tips on Maintaining Engagement Within the Audience

When faced with a disinterested audience, there are several strategies you can employ to re-engage them:

- **Start With a Strong Hook**: Begin your presentation with a compelling story, a thought-provoking question, or a surprising statistic to capture their attention from the start.

- **Use Interactive Elements**: Incorporate audience participation through activities, polls, or Q&A sessions to make them feel involved and invested in the presentation.

- **Vary Your Delivery**: Utilize a mix of storytelling, humor, visuals, and personal anecdotes to keep the audience engaged and interested in your message.

- **Address Their Concerns**: Take a moment to acknowledge their disinterest or skepticism and address any potential objections or doubts they may have. Show that you understand their perspective and provide compelling reasons to stay engaged.

- **Connect on an Emotional Level**: Tap into the audience's emotions by sharing relatable stories or appealing to their values and aspirations. This can help create a deeper connection and rekindle their interest.

- **Adjust Your Pace and Energy**: Be mindful of your delivery speed and energy level. If the audience seems disengaged, consider slowing down, using pauses for emphasis, or injecting more enthusiasm into your voice and body language.

- **Provide Relevance and Benefits**: Clearly communicate the relevance of your topic and how it can benefit the audience. Highlight the value they can gain from listening to your presentation, whether it's new insights, practical tips, or solutions to their challenges.

Remember, engaging a disinterested audience requires adaptability, empathy, and a willingness to adjust your approach. There's always something you can do to increase the chances of capturing their attention and re-engaging them in your presentation.

Look, regardless of what your hopes are or how well-prepared you are, there's always going to be that thing that tries to detail you, but that shouldn't take away from your performance and the value that you can give. So remember that, and don't forget that there is this guide that you can always use. Return to remind yourself of how you can bounce back.

Chapter 7:

Dos and Don'ts to Excel as an

Outstanding Speaker

I know that we've already used a lot of useful tips that will serve you well, but what we really didn't do was put together a thorough list of dos and don'ts to be exemplified as outstanding. Now, I have shared quite a lot of stories throughout the book, and what a shame it would be if I didn't bring that same energy to this chapter? This one takes place in a bustling school auditorium filled with eager students and their proud parents. I took my place as an adjudicator for the public speaking competition. The atmosphere was charged with anticipation, and I couldn't help but feel excited for the young speakers about to take the stage.

As the first contestant approached the microphone, a wave of nervous energy washed over the room. The young girl, brimming with confidence, began her speech with gusto. Alas, there was one small hiccup—she spoke at lightning speed, barely taking a breath between words. Her words tumbled out like a waterfall, leaving the audience bewildered and struggling to keep up. I couldn't help but chuckle inwardly, realizing that this was a classic example of the importance of pacing and clarity in public speaking.

Despite her enthusiasm and well-crafted content, the rapid-fire delivery hindered her ability to effectively connect with the audience. It was as if she had pressed the fast-forward button on her speech, leaving everyone in a state of confusion. The lesson here was clear: speaking too fast can undermine even the most well-prepared presentation. It's crucial to find a balance, allowing your words to flow naturally while giving your audience time to absorb and process the information.

I couldn't help but admire the young girl's courage and determination, though. She had taken a risk, and even though it didn't go as planned, it was a valuable learning experience for her and everyone in the room.

So, remember, there is power in a moment of pause. Take a breath, slow down, and allow your words to sink into the hearts of your audience.

A Big "No"

We're going to start with the no's. Now, you may have content that is fair, but if there are certain things that you do or neglect to do, then you might as well not have given a speech at all. So, from talking too fast to trying to press your beliefs on your students, we're going to unpack all of those things in this chapter.

Don't Impose Your Views on the Audience

I once had a chance encounter with a man who shared a rather peculiar but thought-provoking statement. He said, 'You cannot convince a man who wants to believe that a tangerine is an orange that it actually is a tangerine.' At first, I found this idiom to be amusing, but upon reflection, I realized its profound implications for public speaking.

In the realm of public speaking, we cannot forget that each individual in the audience comes with their own set of beliefs, perspectives, and preconceived notions. As speakers, we must resist the temptation to impose our views forcefully on them. Just like the man who stubbornly insists that a tangerine is an orange, some audience members may hold steadfast to their own convictions, regardless of the evidence presented.

Attempting to change someone's deeply ingrained beliefs through a single speech is a daunting task if not an impossible one. Instead, our goal should be to foster an environment of open-mindedness where ideas can be shared and explored without the pressure to conform. By acknowledging and respecting the diversity of opinions within our audience, we create a space for meaningful dialogue and genuine connection. It is through this exchange of ideas that we can plant seeds of thought, allowing individuals to reflect and potentially reconsider their own perspectives over time.

Rather than forcefully imposing our views, we should strive to present our ideas in a compelling and persuasive manner. By providing well-reasoned arguments, supporting evidence, and relatable anecdotes, we can invite the audience to consider alternative viewpoints without feeling coerced.

Remember, the power of persuasion lies not in forcefully bending others to our will but in inspiring them to think critically and arrive at their own conclusions. You want to respect the beauty that comes from autonomy and individuality, so, as you prepare yourself to step onto the stage, remember the wisdom of the tangerine and the orange.

Avoid Filler Words

Have you ever found yourself in a conversation where someone used complex words or industry jargon that left you feeling confused and disconnected? or thinking, "Am I really that stupid?" I once had a similar experience, and it made me realize the importance of avoiding the use of fuller words in public speaking.

When we approach an audience, our goal should be to communicate our message clearly and effectively. Using unnecessarily complex language or jargon can create a barrier between the speaker and the audience, hindering understanding and engagement.

Imagine trying to explain a concept to someone using technical terms they are unfamiliar with. It's like speaking a foreign language to them. They may nod along, pretending to understand, but in reality, they are left feeling lost and disengaged.

To truly connect with our audience, we must strive for simplicity and clarity in our language. Instead of trying to impress with complex vocabulary, we should aim to convey our ideas in a way that is accessible and relatable to all.

By using plain language, we make our message more inclusive and inviting. We allow our audience to fully grasp the essence of our ideas without the need for a dictionary or specialized knowledge.

Remember, the goal of public speaking is not to showcase our intelligence or vocabulary prowess. It is to effectively communicate our message and connect with our audience on a deeper level. By using simpler language, we create a bridge of understanding that allows our message to resonate with a wider range of individuals.

Examples of Filler Words

- "Um" or "uh:" These are common filler words used when someone is pausing or searching for the right words. They can make the speaker appear less confident or prepared.

- "Like:" This word is often used as a filler when someone is unsure or trying to emphasize a point. Overusing "like" can distract from the main message and make the speaker sound less credible.

- "You know:" This phrase is often used as a way to seek validation or agreement from the audience. However, excessive use can make the speaker sound uncertain or lacking in confidence.

- "Basically:" This word is often used to simplify or summarize a concept. However, when overused, it can make the speaker sound repetitive or diminish the complexity of the topic.

- "So:" This word is often used as a transition or filler when someone is gathering their thoughts. However, excessive use of "so" can make the speech sound disjointed or lacking in structure.

- "Well:" This word is often used as a filler when someone is unsure how to begin a sentence or response. Overusing "well" can make the speaker sound hesitant or unprepared.

- "Actually:" This word is often used to emphasize a point or correct a misconception. However, excessive use can make the speaker sound defensive or create a sense of doubt.

Common Jargon Examples

Some common examples of jargon or technical language can vary depending on the specific field or topic being discussed. However, here are a few general examples:

- **Acronyms**: Using abbreviations or acronyms that may not be familiar to the audience without providing an explanation. For example, using terms like ROI (Return on Investment) or KPIs (Key Performance Indicators) without clarifying their meaning.

- **Technical Terms**: Using specialized terminology that may be specific to a particular industry or field. For instance, using medical terminology in a speech about healthcare without providing clear explanations for nonmedical professionals.

- **Buzzwords**: Utilizing trendy or overused words or phrases that may not have a clear meaning or may be vague. Examples include terms like "synergy," "disruption," or "paradigm shift" without providing context or concrete explanations.

- **Industry-Specific Jargon**: Using language that is commonly understood within a specific profession or field but may be unfamiliar to a broader audience. This could include terms like "SEO" (Search Engine Optimization) in a marketing context or "beta testing" in a technology-related discussion.

Never Rush to Finish

One of the most nerve-racking things that can undoubtedly happen to you as a speaker is realizing that you only have about ten minutes left, and yet you haven't even gotten to the good bits of your speech. What do you do in that moment? Do you turn into the flash and start speaking at the speed of lightning in the hopes that you'll manage to squeeze everything in the nip of that moment, or do you play it cool and try to hide all of that nervousness from your audience? When faced with the realization that time is running out, you have to resist the urge to rush through the remaining content. Instead, take a deep breath and focus on delivering the key points effectively. Rushing can lead to a loss of clarity and comprehension for the audience, defeating the purpose of your speech. By maintaining a calm and composed demeanor, you can ensure that your message is conveyed effectively. Remember, quality over quantity is key in public speaking.

Common Mistakes Made During Time Management in a Speech

- **Not Planning or Rehearsing**: Failing to plan and practice your speech can lead to uncertainty about timing and make it difficult to manage time effectively.

- **Overloading With Content**: Trying to include too much information in your speech can lead to rushing and sacrificing clarity. Focus on the key points and avoid overwhelming your audience.

- **Ignoring Time Limits**: Disregarding time limits set by event organizers or exceeding the allotted time can disrupt the schedule and inconvenience both the audience and other speakers.

- **Lack of Awareness**: Not keeping track of time during your speech can result in going over or under the allocated time. Stay mindful of the clock and adjust your pace accordingly.

- **Poor Transitions**: Failing to plan smooth transitions between different sections of your speech can lead to awkward pauses or unnecessary time wastage.

- **Getting Sidetracked**: Going off on tangents or getting too engrossed in a particular topic can cause you to lose track of time and neglect other important points.

- **Underestimating Audience Engagement**: If you assume your audience will be disinterested or unresponsive, you may rush through your speech, missing opportunities for engagement and interaction.

Tips for Better Time Management During Your Speech

- **Plan and Practice**: Make sure that you create a well-structured outline or script for your speech and rehearse it multiple times to get a sense of timing.

- **Time**: Use a stopwatch or timer during practice sessions to gauge how long each section of your speech takes. This will help you allocate time appropriately during the actual presentation.

- **Prioritize Key Points**: Identify the most important points you want to convey and allocate more time to them. This ensures that even if you run short on time, the essential information is still delivered.

- **Use Visual Aids Wisely**: If you're using slides or other visual aids, make sure they enhance your message without taking up too much time. Keep them concise and focused.

- **Be Mindful of Pace**: Speak at a comfortable and steady pace, allowing your audience to absorb the information. Avoid speaking too quickly or too slowly, as both can hinder comprehension.

- **Practice Transitions**: Smooth transitions between different sections of your speech can help save time. Practice moving seamlessly from one point to another to avoid unnecessary pauses or delays.

- **Have a Backup Plan**: Essentially, this just means preparing for unexpected circumstances, such as technical difficulties or interruptions, by having a condensed version of your speech or key points ready to deliver if needed.

Never Doubt Your Skills

Self-doubt is like that unwelcome guest who shows up unannounced at the most inconvenient of times. It's that nagging voice in your head that makes you question your abilities; it plants seeds of uncertainty and tries to convince you that you're not good enough. It's like having a little devil on your shoulder, constantly whispering doubts and fears into your ear.

Just imagine: There's this dream or a goal you want to pursue, and it's something exciting and meaningful to you. You're all pumped up and ready to take on the world. But then it creeps in and starts asking you questions like, "What if you fail?" or "Who do you think you are to achieve this?"

The thing about self-doubt is that it thrives on fear and insecurity. It feeds on past failures, negative experiences, and the comparisons we make with others. It's like a master illusionist, distorting reality and making you believe that you lack the skills, knowledge, or talent to succeed. It creates this illusion that you are somehow inadequate, and it can be incredibly persuasive. We humans have a natural desire to be accepted and to fit in. We fear rejection or judgment from others, and self-doubt preys on that fear. It convinces us that if we try something new or take a risk, we'll embarrass ourselves or be ridiculed by others. It's like a protective mechanism gone haywire, trying to shield us from potential harm but ultimately holding us back from reaching our full potential.

Most of us also have this unhelpful tendency to compare ourselves to others. In today's digital age, it's so easy to scroll through social media and see people's highlight reels, their successes, and their achievements. We start comparing our own journey to theirs, forgetting that we're only seeing a curated version of their lives. This constant comparison breeds self-doubt as we feel like we're falling short or not measuring up to some unattainable standard.

But here's the thing: It is merely a perception. It's not an accurate reflection of your worth or capabilities. It's a construct of your mind, often based on irrational fears and distorted thinking. The good news is that you have the power to challenge and overcome it, one of the ways being through self-awareness. Pay attention to your thoughts and feelings when self-doubt arises. Question the validity of those doubts and challenge them with evidence of your past accomplishments and strengths. Remind yourself of times when you've overcome challenges and succeeded. Surround yourself with positive and supportive people who believe in you and your abilities.

Additionally, you can take small steps towards your goals. Break them down into manageable tasks, and with each step you take, you build confidence and prove to yourself that you are capable. Celebrate your victories, no matter how small they may seem because they all add up and contribute to your growth.

These moments of doubt and uncertainty are all part of being human. Even the most accomplished individuals have experienced it at some point. It's not about eradicating self-doubt entirely but learning to manage it and not let it hold you back. Embrace the discomfort, acknowledge your fears, and take action anyway.

So, here are a few final comforting reminders that I want you to keep in mind:

- No one can speak or will ever speak like you do. Embrace the beauty that comes from the whole truth.

- Your voice has a purpose. Remember that you have a unique perspective and valuable insights to share. Trust in the importance of your message and the impact it can have on others.

- You don't have to be perfect. No one expects you to be. Understand that nobody expects you to be flawless. Embrace the fact that making mistakes is a natural part of the learning process and can even make your presentation more relatable and authentic.

- Show up and prepare: The more you prepare, the more confident you'll feel. Invest time in research, practice your delivery, and familiarize yourself with your material. Preparation breeds confidence.

- Recall previous speaking engagements or presentations where you felt successful. Remind yourself of your accomplishments and the positive feedback you received. Use those experiences as a source of confidence and motivation.

- Don't forget that it's also about the people you're talking to. Shift your focus from yourself to your audience. Concentrate on providing value, inspiring, educating, or entertaining them. When you prioritize your audience's needs, it helps alleviate self-doubt.

- Welcome, and embrace that nervous energy. Recognize that it's normal to feel nervous before speaking in public. Instead of fighting it, embrace the energy and channel it into enthusiasm and passion for your topic.

- Don't be shy about your accomplishments. Picture yourself delivering your speech with confidence and receiving a positive response from the audience. Visualizing success can help create a positive mindset and reduce self-doubt.

- Be intentional about who you surround yourself with. Surround yourself with supportive individuals who can provide constructive feedback. Seek reassuring comments from trusted friends, colleagues, or mentors who can help boost your confidence.

- Champion yourself and cheer for yourself along the way. Acknowledge and celebrate your growth as a speaker. Recognize that every speaking opportunity, regardless of the outcome, contributes to your development. Give yourself credit for stepping out of your comfort zone.

Self-doubt will always be there, but it's really more about how you respond to it that matters. Use these reminders to build your confidence and embrace the gift of speaking that you possess.

A Must-Do

Be prepared to be flexible. Okay, so you've prepared everything, but you also have to make sure that you leave enough room open for flexibility because anything can happen. You might forget something that you wrote, or there might be a slight interruption that throws you off. You must remember that's okay. Nobody else knows what you practiced in front of the mirror, or nobody else really knows what you meant to say initially, so just going with the flow might actually make you sound more natural than you think.

Don't forget to bring your notes. Sure, you're a great public speaker and all, but even the greatest of public speakers need a little bit of assistance every now and again. What I usually do and what I recommend you do as well is jot down the key 5–10 topics that you'll be talking about. Seeing those little parts of the speech reminds me of the entire speech.

That's it for this chapter, too, and the one thing that I want you to remember is to not be afraid; you don't have to be. Remember that people came to listen to you because they thought you were brilliant.

So, stand with that head held high and be ready to be bold and brilliant. Don't be afraid, because you know what you're talking about. You're the expert.

Chapter 8:

Bust the Misleading Myths

Being a Good Speaker Is an Inborn Talent

Public speaking is often seen as a skill reserved for the chosen few, those who are naturally gifted with the ability to captivate an audience effortlessly. However, the truth is that being a good speaker is not solely an inborn talent. It is a skill that can be learned and developed with practice and dedication.

Think about it this way: Nobody is born knowing how to ride a bicycle. It takes time, effort, and a few falls before we can confidently pedal down the street. Similarly, public speaking is a skill that can be honed through learning and experience.

While some individuals may have a natural inclination towards communication, that doesn't mean they automatically become great speakers. Even the most gifted speakers have to work on their craft to truly excel. They invest time in studying effective communication techniques, refining their delivery, and practicing their speeches.

The key to becoming a good speaker lies in understanding that it's not just about talent but also about preparation and practice. It's about developing the ability to connect with your audience, convey your message clearly, and engage their attention. These skills can be learned and improved upon over time.

So, if you want to become a better speaker, don't be discouraged by the myth that it's all about innate talent. Instead, focus on developing your skills through consistent practice, seeking feedback, and learning from experienced speakers. With dedication and perseverance, anyone can become a confident and effective public speaker, regardless of their natural abilities.

Experience Reduces Nervousness

Public speaking can be an anxiety-inducing activity for many people, regardless of their level of experience. Even seasoned speakers can still feel a level of nervousness before stepping onto the stage. The difference lies in how they handle and channel that nervous energy.

Experience can provide speakers with valuable insights and strategies to cope with nervousness. They may have developed techniques to calm their nerves, such as deep breathing exercises or visualization. They might have learned to reframe their anxiety as excitement, harnessing that energy to deliver a more dynamic presentation.

However, it's important to note that nervousness can still persist, especially in new or challenging speaking situations. Each speaking engagement is unique, and even experienced speakers can encounter unfamiliar audiences or topics that trigger nerves.

The key is not to expect nervousness to completely disappear with experience but rather to embrace it as a natural part of the process. With practice and exposure, speakers can become more comfortable and confident, but that doesn't mean they won't experience any nerves at all.

So, while experience can certainly help in managing and mitigating nervousness, it's important to recognize that it's a continuous journey. Embrace the nerves, use them to your advantage, and keep refining your skills as a speaker. With time and practice, you can become more adept at handling nervousness and delivering impactful presentations.

Introverts Cannot Become Good Speakers

The notion that introverts cannot become good public speakers is a myth that fails to recognize the unique strengths and qualities introverted individuals bring to the table. In fact, introverts can excel in public speaking and captivate audiences just as effectively as their extroverted counterparts. Here's why:

- **Preparation and Thoughtfulness**: Introverts are known for their reflective nature and inclination towards deep thinking. These qualities can be advantageous in public speaking. Introverts often invest time and effort into researching, organizing their thoughts, and crafting well-structured speeches. Their meticulous preparation allows them to deliver compelling and meaningful presentations that resonate with the audience.

- **Authenticity and Depth**: Introverts tend to be introspective and value authenticity. When speaking in public, they bring a genuine and sincere approach that connects with listeners on a deeper level. Introverts often share personal stories, insights, and perspectives that touch the audience's emotions and create a lasting impact. Their ability to convey vulnerability and authenticity can make their speeches incredibly compelling and relatable.

- **Active Listening and Empathy:** Introverts are skilled listeners. They possess the ability to keenly observe and understand the needs and reactions of their audience. This empathetic nature enables them to tailor their speeches to the specific interests and concerns of the listeners. By actively listening and being attuned to the audience's cues, introverts can engage and connect with their listeners effectively, fostering a sense of trust and engagement.

- **Power of Preparation**: Introverts often excel in one-on-one or small group interactions. This strength can be honed to their advantage in public speaking. Through thorough preparation, introverts can harness their expertise on the topic, anticipate potential questions or objections, and deliver well-informed responses. This level of preparation instills confidence, allowing introverts to navigate challenging situations during presentations or Q&A sessions with poise and composure.

- **Compelling Communication Style**: While introverts may not possess the overt charisma associated with extroverts, they have a unique communication style that is captivating in its own right. Introverts tend to be thoughtful speakers, choosing their words carefully and delivering messages with precision and impact. Their calm and composed demeanor can draw the audience's attention, creating an atmosphere of attentiveness and receptiveness.

It Is Impossible to Overcome Public Fear

And another myth that usually stops people from going out there to reach their full potential, but the reality as it is, is that many people have successfully overcome their fear and become confident and engaging public speakers. Allow me to provide you with an engaging explanation as to why this myth is simply not true.

- **Desensitization**: Fear of public speaking is often rooted in a fear of judgment or criticism from others. One effective way to overcome this fear is through desensitization, which involves gradually exposing oneself to public speaking situations. By starting with small groups or familiar audiences and gradually increasing the size and complexity of speaking engagements, individuals can become more comfortable and build confidence over time.

- **Preparation and Practice**: Another key aspect of overcoming the fear of public speaking is thorough preparation and practice. When individuals feel well-prepared and have a deep understanding of their topic, they are more likely to feel confident and less anxious while speaking in front of others.

Proper practice also helps individuals become familiar with their material, allowing for a smoother and more engaging delivery.

- **Visualization and Positive Thinking**: Harnessing the power of visualization and positive thinking can significantly aid in overcoming the fear of public speaking. By visualizing successful outcomes and positive reactions from the audience, individuals can shift their mindset from anxiety and fear to confidence and success. This technique helps them approach public speaking with a more positive and constructive mindset.

- **Seeking Support and Feedback**: It's important to acknowledge that public speaking can be a daunting task, but it doesn't have to be faced alone. Seeking support from mentors, joining public speaking clubs or groups, or participating in workshops can provide valuable feedback and guidance. Constructive criticism and encouragement from others can help individuals identify and address areas for improvement, further boosting their confidence as public speakers.

- **Embracing Mistakes as Learning Opportunities**: Public speaking is a skill that can be continuously improved over time. It's essential to embrace mistakes as valuable learning opportunities rather than allowing them to intensify fear. By reframing mistakes as stepping stones to growth and improvement, individuals can maintain a positive attitude and make progress in their public speaking journey.

Remember, the fear of public speaking is not an insurmountable hurdle. With the right mindset, preparation, practice, support, and a commitment to growth, anyone can overcome this fear and become an engaging and confident public speaker.

Practice Can Improve Speaking Skills

You've heard the age-old advice that practice makes perfect, so you've spent hours rehearsing your speech, hoping it will magically transform you into a captivating speaker. But here's the truth: the myth that practice alone can improve your public speaking skills is just that—a myth.

Don't get me wrong, practice is essential. It helps you become familiar with your content, fine-tune your delivery, and build confidence. However, public speaking is not just about reciting words flawlessly. It's about connecting with your audience, engaging their attention, and leaving a lasting impact. And that requires more than just practice.

Think about it this way: If you were learning to play the piano, would practicing scales alone make you a great pianist? Probably not. You would also need to understand music theory, develop a sense of rhythm, and learn to interpret and express emotions through your playing. Similarly, public speaking is an art that encompasses various elements.

To truly excel in public speaking, you need to understand your audience. Are they young professionals, industry experts, or students? Tailoring your speech to their needs and interests is crucial. What are their pain points, desires, or challenges? By empathizing with your audience, you can craft a message that resonates with them on a deeper level.

Communication skills are another vital aspect of public speaking. It's not just about what you say but how you say it. Are you using vocal variety, gestures, and body language to enhance your message? Are you maintaining eye contact and projecting confidence? These skills can't be honed through practice alone; they require conscious effort and continuous improvement.

Lastly, adaptability is key. No two audiences are the same, so being able to adjust your approach on the fly is essential. Are they engaged and responsive? Great! Keep up the energy. Are they looking bored or confused? It's time to switch gears, ask questions, or add some humor to re-engage them.

So, while practice is an important piece of the puzzle, it's not the sole answer to becoming a great public speaker. Understanding your audience, developing strong communication skills, and being adaptable are equally vital.

Chapter 9:

Extraordinary Public Speakers

Around the World

We all get our inspiration from somewhere, and most of it comes from seeing people do the things that we want to do. When it comes to the art of public speaking, there are extraordinary individuals around the world who have captivated audiences, leaving an indelible mark on our hearts and minds. These remarkable people have not only mastered the art of effective communication, but they possess a unique ability to touch the deepest recesses of our souls.

One such extraordinary speaker is Malala Yousafzai, the young Pakistani activist who defied the Taliban's oppressive regime to fight for girls' education. Her unwavering determination and bravery in the face of adversity serve as a beacon of hope for millions worldwide. When Malala speaks, her words resonate with a passion that cuts through cultural barriers, reminding us of the power of education and the importance of standing up for what we believe in.

Another exceptional speaker who has left an indomitable impact is Nick Vujicic, an Australian-born motivational speaker born without limbs. Despite facing unimaginable physical challenges, Nick has transformed his own life and inspired countless others to embrace their uniqueness and overcome obstacles. His infectious zest for life and his ability to radiate joy through his words have the power to uplift even the most disheartened souls, reminding us that our limitations need not define us.

In the realm of leadership and personal development, Simon Sinek stands out as a voice that resonates deeply. His TED Talk on the concept of "Start with Why" has garnered millions of views, igniting a global movement centered around finding purpose and meaning in our lives and work. Simon's ability to distill complex ideas into simple yet profound messages has made him a sought-after speaker, reminding us of the importance of aligning our actions with our values.

And who can forget the late Maya Angelou, the renowned American poet and civil rights activist? Maya's eloquent words and powerful presence stirred the souls of listeners, transcending racial and cultural boundaries. With her poignant insights into the human experience, she reminded us of the power of resilience, love, and the beauty of embracing our true selves.

These extraordinary public speakers, and countless others like them, have the ability to awaken something deep within us. They remind us of our shared humanity, our capacity for greatness, and the transformative power of words. Through their stories, they inspire us to overcome our fears, chase our dreams, and make a positive difference in the world. In this chapter, we get to learn more about people like these, who they are, and what exactly it is that makes them so great at what they do.

Christopher Paul Gardner

Christopher Paul Gardner is an American entrepreneur, motivational speaker, and philanthropist. His inspiring life story, depicted in the film "The Pursuit of Happiness," has made him a captivating public speaker. His authenticity, resilience, and ability to connect emotionally with his audience are the key factors that make him extraordinary.

The one thing that stands out, and what we can learn from him, is the power of storytelling. He masterfully weaves his personal experiences into his speeches, allowing his listeners to relate to and empathize with his journey. By sharing his triumphs and struggles, he creates a genuine connection that resonates with his audience.

Another important aspect of Gardner's speaking style is his ability to infuse humor into his talks. He uses light-hearted anecdotes and witty remarks to engage his audience and keep them entertained. This approach helps to create a relaxed and enjoyable atmosphere, making it easier for listeners to connect with the message he is delivering.

Gardner also emphasizes the importance of authenticity. He encourages us to be true to ourselves and speak from the heart because, ultimately, that is how indelible marks are made on the hearts of our readers.

Oprah Winfrey

When it comes to powerful speakers, Oprah Winfrey is undoubtedly an inspiring figure to learn from. Her ability to engage, connect, and empower her audience sets her apart as a masterful communicator.

First and foremost, her authenticity shines through in her speeches. She fearlessly shares her personal stories, vulnerabilities, and triumphs, allowing her audience to relate to her on a deeply human level. Like Brené Brown, Oprah understands the power of vulnerability in forging meaningful connections. She invites her listeners to embrace their own imperfections and feel a sense of belonging.

Another key aspect of Oprah's speaking prowess is her ability to convey empathy. She possesses a remarkable capacity to understand and empathize with the struggles, dreams, and aspirations of her audience. This empathetic approach enables her to speak directly to the hearts of individuals from diverse backgrounds.

Oprah Winfrey's storytelling skills are also worth highlighting. She possesses an incredible talent for crafting narratives that are not only captivating but also imbued with profound meaning. Her stories are often deeply personal and infused with lessons learned from her own life experiences. Through her storytelling, Oprah creates a sense of shared experience, offering her audience valuable insights and inspiring them to reflect on their own journeys.

One more quality that sets Oprah apart is her ability to inspire action. She goes beyond merely delivering motivational speeches; she actively encourages her listeners to make positive changes in their lives and in the world. Her speeches often have a call-to-action component, whether it be promoting literacy, advocating for social justice, or encouraging personal growth. Oprah's ability to ignite a sense of purpose and mobilize her audience to take tangible steps toward their goals is a testament to her exceptional persuasive skills.

Brené Brown

Brené Brown is a mesmerizing speaker whose work on vulnerability, courage, and resilience has resonated with millions of people worldwide.

Her authenticity is a hallmark of her speaking style. She brings her whole self to the stage, sharing her own vulnerabilities and struggles without hesitation. This authenticity creates an immediate connection with her audience, as it allows them to see themselves reflected in her stories and experiences. As aspiring speakers, we can learn from her by embracing our own authenticity and being willing to show up as our genuine selves, even with our imperfections.

She also possesses an uncanny ability to convey complex concepts in a relatable and accessible manner. She combines research, personal anecdotes, and storytelling to distill profound insights into practical and understandable messages. Her ability to communicate complex ideas with clarity and simplicity is a valuable skill for any public speaker. It reminds us to strive for clarity in our own presentations, ensuring that our audience can easily grasp and internalize our messages.

Brown's vulnerability is also a tremendous strength that we can learn from. She courageously shares her own stories of shame, failure, and growth, demonstrating that vulnerability is not a weakness but a source of strength. By being vulnerable, she creates a safe space for her audience to explore their own emotions, fears, and aspirations. As aspiring speakers, we can learn from her to embrace vulnerability as a means to connect deeply with our audience and foster an environment of trust and authenticity.

Importantly, her speeches are rooted in empathy and compassion. She has a deep understanding of the human experience and demonstrates genuine care for her audience. This empathy allows her to connect with people on an emotional level and create a sense of belonging. As speakers, we can learn from her by cultivating empathy, actively listening to our audience, and acknowledging their experiences and emotions.

Lastly, Brown's ability to inspire action sets her apart as a powerful speaker. She not only shares insights and stories but also motivates her audience to take ownership of their lives and make positive changes. Her talks often include practical strategies and tools that empower individuals to embrace vulnerability, cultivate resilience, and live more wholeheartedly. As aspiring speakers, we can learn from her to incorporate actionable steps and calls to action in our own speeches, encouraging our audience to translate inspiration into tangible results.

Tony Robbins

Tony Ribbons possesses a commanding presence on stage. His body language, posture, and overall demeanor exude confidence and authority. This presence immediately grabs the attention of the audience, making them eager to listen to what he has to say. He is also a master storyteller. He knows how to weave compelling narratives, anecdotes, and personal experiences into his speeches, making them relatable and memorable for the audience.

Robbins is a master of delivering his message in a clear and concise manner. He avoids unnecessary jargon or complex language, ensuring that his audience can easily comprehend his ideas. We can learn from him the importance of simplicity and clarity in our own speeches, as it helps to keep the audience engaged and interested.

He also understands the power of visual aids and props to enhance his speeches. He effectively incorporates slides, props, or visual aids to support his message and make it more memorable.

Engaging the Audience: Ribbons actively engages his audience throughout his speeches. He encourages participation, asks thought-provoking questions, or uses humor to keep the audience involved and interested. Through this, he teaches us the importance of creating two-way communication with their audience, fostering engagement and interaction.

Conclusion

As we reach the end of our journey together, it's time to reflect on the incredible transformation you've undergone. From the early stages of uncertainty to the newfound confidence that radiates from within, you have conquered the art of public speaking. The time has come to unleash the power of your voice and share your message with the world.

Throughout this book, we have explored the fundamental principles that form the foundation of effective public speaking. We discovered the importance of thorough preparation, understanding our audience, and crafting compelling narratives that resonate deeply. We delved into the art of body language, the nuances of vocal delivery, and the subtle power of persuasive techniques. Above all, we recognized the immense potential that resides within each of us to connect, inspire, and influence others through the spoken word.

Remember, public speaking is not solely about honing a skill; it is about embracing your authentic self. It is about stepping into the spotlight with unwavering confidence, allowing your passion and knowledge to shine through. It is about understanding that your voice has the power to move mountains, change lives, and ignite revolutions.

As you embark on your own speaking journey, keep in mind that every great orator started somewhere. They faced their fears and stumbled along the way but never lost sight of their vision. They embraced failure as a stepping stone to success and persevered through the darkest moments. They understood that true growth comes when we step outside our comfort zones and embrace the unknown.

Go forth and conquer the stages, boardrooms, and auditoriums that await you. Embrace the nerves as a sign of your readiness to make an impact. Remember the lessons you've learned, the tools you've acquired, and the stories you've crafted. But most importantly, never forget the power of your voice and the ability it possesses to inspire, educate, and provoke change.

References

Barnard, D. (2017, August 18). *What are the benefits of public speaking?* VirtualSpeech. https://virtualspeech.com/blog/what-are-the-benefits-of-public-speaking

Bennetch, R., Owen, C., & Keesey, Z. (2021). *Chapter 33: Methods of speech delivery.* Openpress. https://openpress.usask.ca/rcm200/chapter/types-of-speeches/

Brian Tracey International. (n.d.). *Methods of speech delivery | Public speaking.* Lumen. https://courses.lumenlearning.com/wm-publicspeaking/chapter/methods-of-speech-delivery/

Brian Tracy. (2012, May 1). *Principles of effective public speaking.* https://www.briantracy.com/blog/personal-success/effective-communication-public-speaking-and-presentation-skills/

Brown, M. (n.d.). *What are the problems of public speaking?* Pen and the Pad. https://penandthepad.com/info-8247710-problems-public-speaking.html

Communication skills: ABC principle. (n.d.). Corporate Coach Group. https://corporatecoachgroup.com/blog/communication-skills-abc-principle

Conquering the challenges of public speaking. (n.d.). Skillsoft. https://www.skillsoft.com/course/conquering-the-challenges-of-public-speaking-562bd182-fea5-11e6-8638-0242c0a80b06

Effective speaking skills | Principles, components of effective speaking. (n.d.). XSoftSkills. https://www.xsoftskills.com/2020/03/how-to-develop-effective-speaking-skills.html

Eight-essential-traits-of-successful-public-speakers. (n.d.). Walden University. https://www.waldenu.edu/programs/communication/resourc e/eight-essential-traits-of-successful-public-speakers

5 reasons why is public speaking important? (n.d.). 98thpercentile. https://www.98thpercentile.com/blog/why-is-public-speaking-important/

Hammoud, M. (n.d.). *The ABCs of clear communication.* LinkedIn. https://www.linkedin.com/pulse/abcs-clear-communication-mohamed-hammoud/

Johnson, S. (n.d.). *7 of the greatest public speakers in history.* Big Think. https://bigthink.com/high-culture/7-of-the-greatest-public-speakers-in-history/

McGuire, C. (n.d.). *Essential qualities of a great public speaker.* Ethos3. https://ethos3.com/essential-qualities-of-a-great-public-speaker/

Mind Tools Content Team. (2022). *The 7 Cs of communication.* Mindtools. https://www.mindtools.com/a5xap8q/the-7-cs-of-communication

Morgan, N. (2017, May 11). *Principles of public speaking - I.* Public Words. https://publicwords.com/2017/05/11/principles-public-speaking/

Mustapha, I. (2019, March 20). *Four types of public speaking delivery.* LinkedIn. https://www.linkedin.com/pulse/four-types-public-speaking-delivery-ibrahim-mustapha/

PAN Communications. (n.d.). *3 reasons why public speaking is important.* https://www.pancommunications.com/insights/3-reasons-why-public-speaking-is-important/

Principles of public speaking | Simple book production. (n.d.). Lumen. https://courses.lumenlearning.com/publicspeakingprinciples/

Sinusoid, D. (2021, February 25). *The 9 principles of public speaking from Carmine Gallo.* Shortform Books. https://www.shortform.com/blog/principles-of-public-speaking/

Soni, A. (n.d.). *7 of the greatest public speakers in history.* Big Think. https://bigthink.com/high-culture/7-of-the-greatest-public-speakers-in-history/

Spencer, L. (2021a, August 4). *What are the life-changing benefits of public speaking?* Business Envato Tuts+. https://business.tutsplus.com/articles/benefits-of-public-speaking--cms-30694

Spencer, L. (2021b, August 4). *What are the life-changing benefits of public speaking?* Business Envato Tuts+. https://business.tutsplus.com/articles/benefits-of-public-speaking--cms-30694

Staneart, D. (2019, March 17). *7 qualities of a good public speaker that every presenter should know (and emulate).* Fearless. https://www.fearlesspresentations.com/7-qualities-of-a-good-public-speaker-that-every-presenter-should-know-and-emulate/

Tuttar, J. (2023, April 25). *The 5Ps of public speaking.* Speak & conquer. https://speakandconquer.com/the-5ps-of-public-speaking/

What are the benefits of public speaking? (n.d.). Iglobal Academy. https://iglobal-ac.net/what-are-the-benefits-of-publicspeaking

What is effective communication? Skills for work, school, and life. (2023, February 16). Coursera. https://www.coursera.org/articles/communication-effectiveness

Why is public speaking important? It's useful. (2020, February 9). University of the People. https://www.uopeople.edu/blog/why-is-public-speaking-important/

Zeoli, R. (2019a). *Seven principles of effective public speaking.* Amanet.org. https://www.amanet.org/articles/seven-principles-of-effective-public-speaking/

Printed in Great Britain
by Amazon